►► guide contents

2014 USA & Canada Hostels & Travel Guide

Published by:
Bakpak Travelers Guide, Inc.
PO BOX 10954
Marina Del Rey, CA 90295
Ph/Fax 718.504.5099
info@bakpakguide.com
www.bakpakguide.com

Publisher & Editor
David Barish

Advertising Sales
David Barish

For an advertising media kit, please send an email to:
sales@bakpakguide.com

Cover Design
Lina Tuv/Tallina Design

Photo Credits
Aleksandar Kolundzija (cover), Michael Valdez (cover), ImagineGolf (cover), bubbalove (pg 16), Can Balcioglu (pg 24), Aaron Kohr (pg 26), Harris Shiffman (pg 33), P_Wei (pg 34), Missing35mm (pg 38), Adam Booth (pg 39), ajphoto (pg40), carterdayne (pg 42), cosmonaut (pg 44), Don Croswhite (pg 45), drbueller (pg 46), Heather Shimmin (pg 55), Adam Booth (pg 56), Roberto A Sanchez (pg 58), zennie (pg 64), Sangfoto (pg 68)

Distribution Requests
distribution@bakpakguide.com

Updates/Corrections
Please send listing requests, updates, stories or corrections to: updates@bakpakguide.com

www.facebook.com/bakpakguide

» travel essentials

Welcome to Bakpak's 17th edition of the USA/Canada Hostels & Travel Guide. The Guide is broken down into easy sections to help you plan an unforgettable adventure. Along with the best ways to get around the US and Canada, you will find info on the most popular cities and destinations.

I've also included tons of money saving tips, free things to see & do, maps for major cities and even some must do activities. So be safe and have a blast. Happy Travels from Bakpak Dave!

DIGITAL GUIDE

Bakpak also offers a digital version of our USA/Canada Hostels & Travel Guide. You can view or download the online Guide by visiting our website, www.bakpakguide.com

With the digital version, you can print pages, save it to your computer and best of all, click on the website links and ads in the guide. Please share it with you friends and Like it on Facebook.

GETTING AROUND

There are no shortage of options for getting around the US and Canada. Ground transportation includes backpacker tours and hop-on, hop-off passes (see page 14) as well as coach and rail travel (see sections below).

If you want to go at your own pace, check out the many car, camper and campervan rental options for (see page 16).

For the long-haul, there are a number of budget airlines that can get you cross-country from $300 round-trip including Virgin America, Southwest and Jet Blue.

Rail Travel

The following are the national rail companies for the US and Canada. While rail travel can be fun and scenic, unfortunately, it is not the cheapest option available for backpackers.

Amtrak (USA)
(800) 872-7245/www.amtrak.com

Via Rail (Canada)
(888) 842-7245/www.viarail.com

Coach Travel

Megabus
(877) 462-6342
www.megabus.com
See their ad on pages 35 & 51

Explore the East Coast, West Coast and the Midwest with Megabus. They operate low cost, express bus services with fares as low as $1. Travel between New York and Boston, Philadelphia, Baltimore, Washington DC, Niagara Falls and Toronto. And between Chicago and Midwest destinations. They now service Southern California as well. Travel on their Double Deck, WiFi equipped coaches from city to city.

Greyhound Lines
(800) 231-2222
www.greyhound.com
See their ad to the right

Greyhound offers coach service across the US and Canada, including express service between many popular cities. You can book online and get web only discounted fares. Please note that Greyhound no longer offers Discovery Passes for international travelers.

Airport Transport

SuperShuttle
(800) 258-3826
www.supershuttle.com
See their ad on the back cover

Get 10% off your ride to/from airports in LA, NYC, Miami, San Fran, DC and more. Use discount code 8WPG4.

Newark Airport Express
www.newarkairportexpress.com
See their ad on page 52

Save $2 off a one-way ticket from Newark Airport to Manhattan or save $5 off a round-trip ticket. Use their coupon on page 52.

TRAVEL INSURANCE

It's always a good idea to have basic backpacker travel insurance in case you get sick, are injured or just lose your bags. You can buy insurance in weekly or monthly increments. And, you can even buy it after your trip has started! Bakpak Dave has partnered with one of the leading backpacker travel insurance companies. For more info, go to www.bakpakguide.com/travelinsurance

BOOKING HOSTELS

Browse the listings, hostel ads and maps with hostel locations in our guide. They provide info on hostel locations, amenities, freebies and contact info (phone, email, web address). Typical hostel amenities include dorms with shared bath, lockers, no curfews, internet/WiFi, common areas, tea/coffee, tour bookings and free breakfast. Many hostels offer private rooms with shared or private bath.

You can book directly with hostels online or by phone to get the best availability and pricing. You can also use the cool hostel booking app from WeHostels (see their ad on page 13).

GENERAL INFO

Money & Banks

are everywhere including grocery stores and supermarkets. Try to avoid non-bank ATM machines (fraud issues). Bank hours vary but are open to at least 4pm, often to 6pm and on Saturdays too.

Electricity

The US and Canada operate on the 110 volt system, not the 220 volt. For global electronics such as your mobile phone, laptop or tablet, you simply need an adapter to convert the plug type.

Tipping & Sales Tax

Tipping is expected from the taxi driver to wait staff (10-20%, avg 15%) depending on the quality of the service.

Vancouver Island
Whistler
VANCOUVER pg 64
Banff
Saskatoon
Nanaimo
Victoria
Calgary
Seattle Port Angeles
Kelowna
Nelson
Fernie
CANADA
Regina
WASHINGTON
Mt. Rainier NP
Spokane
Seaside
Mt. St Helens
MONTANA
Great Falls Missouri
NORTH DAKOTA
Gra
PORTLAND pg 44
Mt. Hood
Bismarck
Fa
Eugene
Butte
OREGON
IDAHO
Bozeman
SOUTH DAKOTA
Crater Lake NP
Boise
Eureka
Idaho Falls
Yellowstone NP
Deadwood
Jackson
Badlands NP
Mt. Rushmore
WYOMING
NORTH CAL pg 33
Reno
Salt Lake City
Sioux City
Sacramento
Cheyenne
NEBRASKA
Omaha
NEVADA
Lincoln
SAN FRAN pg 42
Yosemite NP
Boulder
Monterey
Death Valley NP
Denver
Big Sur
Cedar City
UTAH
Moab
CALIFORNIA
LAS VEGAS pg 39
Bryce Canyon
COLORADO
COAST pg 33
Zion NP
CALIFORNIA
KANSAS
Santa Barbara
Colorado
GRAND CANYON pg 40
Dodge City
Wichit
LOS ANGELES pg 26
Big Bear Lake
FLAGSTAFF pg 40
Santa Fe
Joshua Tree NP
Huntington Beach
ARIZONA
OKLAHOMA
SAN DIEGO pg 34
Albuquerque
Amarillo
Oklahoma
Tijuana
Phoenix
NEW MEXICO
City
Ensenada
Erendira
Roswell
Pacific
Tucson
Ocean
Carlsbad
Dallas
Te
El Paso
TEXAS
BAJA CALIFORNIA pg 38
Austin
Hermosillo
San Antonio
Chihuahua
MEXICO
Rio Grande
Saltillo
Monterrey
Cabo San Lucas

ALASKA
Barrow
HAWAII
Fort Yukon
YUKON
Kauai
Nome
Fairbanks
Oahu
Molokai
Denali NP
Maui
Anchorage
Talkeetna
Whitehorse
BC
Unalaska
Juneau
Big Island
Prince Rupert
0   500 Miles
0   100 Miles
0   500 Km
0   100 Km

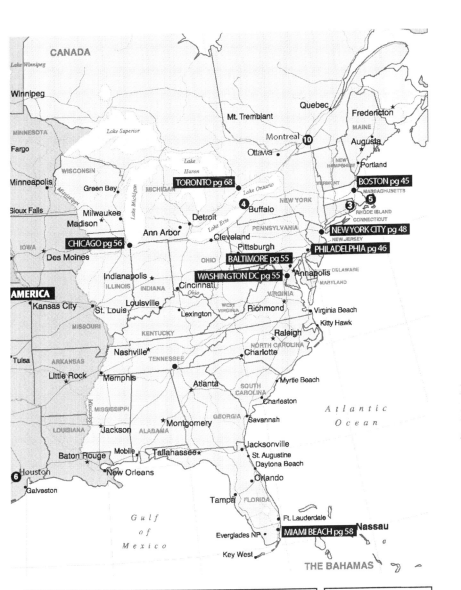

Distance Legend

Los Angeles to New Orleans	1915 miles/3090km
New Orleans to Miami	860 miles/1325km
Los Angeles to San Antonio	1370 miles/2210km
San Francisco to New York	2950 miles/4760km
San Francisco to Chicago	2150 miles/3470km
Seattle to Boston	3090 miles/4985km
Vancouver to Toronto	2780 miles/4485km
Vancouver to Calgary	610 miles/985km
Toronto to New York	500 miles/800km

1 mile=
1.6 km

1km=
.6 miles

Hostel Numbers Index

1 to **6**
page 24

7 to **10**
page 60

⟩⟩ popular trip ideas

North America is a big continent with endless routes and roads to explore it, unlike Australia where there is basically one road north and one west when you arrive in Sydney. So Bakpak Dave has put together a sampling of the most popular routes and trip ideas for your next travel adventure.

1) Southwest's Best

The great American Southwest is a land of iconic red rock vistas, breathtaking canyons, peaceful deserts, exciting lake resorts and beautiful national parks for you to discover. Take some time to explore this area of the country, one of the last uncharted, unfenced, un-pinned down areas left in the wild. This itinerary takes you along the historic Route 66 and through four western states: California, Arizona, Utah and Nevada. Welcome to the Old West.

Route and Trip Length

Los Angeles to Grand Canyon Region to Las Vegas to San Francisco and back to Los Angeles along the coast (see below) or start in San Francisco and take the reverse route.

Highlights & Activities...

Los Angeles, Hollywood, Sin City, Barstow outlet malls, Joshua Tree NP, Grand Canyon National Park, Bryce Canyon, Zion NP, Yosemite, wine country, Big Sur.

How to See it...

Campervan Rental - from $59/day, page 16 (Escape Campervans, Jucy Campervans, Wicked Campers, Lost Campers); **Car Rental** - from $299/week, page 16 (SuperCheap Car, All-States Car Rental, Advance Car Rental); **Adventure Tours** - from $300, page 14 (Trek America, Contiki, Screaming Eagle; **Day Tours** - Southwest Adventures (pg 32), A Day in LA Tours (pg 32), LA City Tours (pg 70), Grand Canyon Hostel Tours (pg 71); **Transport** - pg 4 (Greyhound, Megabus).

< Southwest's Best

California Coast >

2) California Coast

The drive up Highway 1 AKA the Pacific Coast Highway (PCH) is one of the most beautiful in the world and highlights the many reasons California is so loved: brilliant blue ocean waves, near-perfect climate, funky surf towns, breathtaking scenery, marine life and soft sandy beaches.

Whatever you do, don't rush this trip. Although you can drive the 485 miles in a day in a half, rushing your trip on the PCH misses the point completely. Relax - you're in California!

Route and Trip Length

Los Angeles to San Francisco or vice versa. 5-7 days highly recommended.

Highlights & Activities...

Santa Barbara, Santa Cruz, Hearst Castle, whale watching, learn to surf, farmer's markets, old Spanish missions, Santa Inez wine country, sand dunes, tide pools, windy roads.

How to See it...

Campervan Rental - from $59/day, page 16 (Escape Campervans, JUCY Campervans, Wicked Campers, Lost Campers); **Car Rental** - from $299/week, page 16 (Super-Cheap Car, All-States Car Rental, Advanced Car Rental); **Adventure Tours** - from $300, page 14 (Trek America, Contiki, Screaming Eagle; **Transport** - pg 4 (Greyhound, Megabus).

SEE THE BEST OF USA & CANADA

ONE LIFE, ONE SHOT, MAKE IT COUNT!

MENTION "BAKPAK DAVE" TO SAVE $100!*

CHOOSE FROM OVER 20 TRIPS IN USA & CANADA AT CONTIKI.COM

THE ORIGINAL SINCE '62

Use promo code BAKPAKDAVE100 to save $100 when booking any tour 10+ days. Call 1-800-CONTIKI or visit us at Contiki.com to book.

3) Northeast USA

This route is a combination of two popular routes and offers heaps of East Coast experience along with a good dose of fun, games, beaches and harbors. From the eye-popping nightlife of New York City to sobering memorials steeped in early American colonial history. You will visit Boston, Philadelphia - the City of Brotherly Love - as well as the cultural center of Baltimore on your way to Washington DC, just 4-5 hours south of the Big Apple. From Washington DC, instead of going back to New York, you can head south towards Florida.

Route and Trip Length

Washington DC is only 4-5 hours south of New York City along I-95. The first stop is Philadelphia, just 1.5 hours into the trip. However, if you want to check out Atlantic City and the Jersey Shore (Wildwood and Cape May), take the Garden State Parkway from New York first and catch the Atlantic City Expressway into Philly. From there take I-95 south and stop in Baltimore before continuing on to Washington DC.

Highlights & Activities...

Visit the center of the universe, New York City. Stroll in gigantic Central Park, act like a kid at world-famous toy store FAO Schwarz, and pay your respects to the Statue of Liberty and the thousands of immigrants who passed through Ellis Island. Steep yourself in New England history and clam chowder in Boston. Let the juice from a Philly cheese steak drip off your chin in front of the Liberty Bell in Benjamin Franklin's Philadelphia. Dine at a historic restaurant in Baltimore's Inner Harbor then stroll the National Mall in Washington DC. Don't forget to let loose and go wild in the fun-lover's Mecca of Atlantic City. Come on, seven!

How to See it...

Car or Campervan Rental - from $25/day or $179/week, page 16 (Adventures on Wheels, Escape Campervans); **Small Group Adventure Tours** - from $300, page 14 (Trek America, Contiki) **Coach** page 4 (Greyhound, Megabus).

4) Cross-Country USA

There are a number of ways to travel the 3000 miles across the USA. The most popular routes are covered here.

New York and San Francisco

This route takes you through the northern part of the USA from the Big Apple to San Francisco along interstate I-80, passing through the southern part of the Midwest and smack into the heartland, skirting the top of Colorado to reach the Pacific Ocean - a quintessential road trip.

Discover your inner rock star at the Rock and Roll Hall of Fame in Cleveland. Try to eat a whole deep-dish pizza in Chicago. Check out Frank Lloyd Wright's estate, Taliesin, near Madison, and then fill up on hearty heartland fare at one of the city's famous diners. Travel through the open fields and farmland of Iowa and Nebraska and share the

< Northeast USA

road with a buffalo at Yellowstone National Park in Wyoming. Hit the slopes outside of Salt Lake City. Win a nickel jackpot in Reno. Take your first glimpse of the Pacific Ocean from the hills of San Francisco, as explorers have done for centuries, then relax and indulge in a fat night out - you made it!

Atlanta/Miami and Los Angeles

This trip includes four of Bakpak's Top 10 Party Places in America and takes you from the hopping "HOTlanta" down towards the Gulf of Mexico and skirts the southern portion of the States using interstate I-10. Take a detour into and around Florida from Atlanta before heading west.

Highlights include Atlanta, Chattanooga, Mobile, Biloxi, New Orleans, Houston, San Antonio, Austin, Carlsbad Caverns, White Sands National Monument, Roswell, El Paso, Phoenix, Joshua Tree National Park and Palm Springs.

Boston and Seattle

This trip takes you from the eastern seaport of Boston to the majestic mountains of Seattle along interstate I-90, with loads of destinations and activities along the way. Once you've explored Boston, Cape Cod and Nantucket, you are ready to set off on your cross-country adventure.

Steep yourself in New England history and clam chowder in Boston. Go fishing on Lake Erie and go nuts at the roller coaster capital of the world, Cedar Point Amusement Park. Take an Obama tour of America's great city of Chicago. Check out the nightlife in Madison. Ride a horse through Badlands National Park, and imagine yours as the next face on Mt. Rushmore. Spend an afternoon with ghosts of gunslingers of the Old West in Deadwood, and party with the students in Bozeman. Share breakfast with Old Faithful in Yellowstone National Park, and finally arrive in Seattle where you can kayak on Puget Sound, watch the sun set over the Olympic Mountains, and throw a fish at Pike Place Market.

Car or Campervan Rental - from $50/day page 16 (Adventures on Wheels, Escape Campervans); **Small Group Adventure Tours** - from $300, page 14 (Trek America, Contiki); **Coach** - pg 3 ((Greyhound, Megabus).

WINNER
BEST HOSTEL CHAIN 2013
 by HOSTELWORLD.com
☆ 11th Annual Hostel Awards ☆

Why stay anywhere else?

Hollywood
800-524-6783

San Diego
800-438-8622

San Francisco
877-483-2950

www.usahostels.com

5) Best of the West – Vancouver to Calgary

This itinerary follows through the spectacular western part of Canada, starting at the drippy green city of Vancouver and taking you through a few gigantic National Parks with mind-blowing scenery before dropping you back at Calgary. You can also do a side trip to Vancouver Island before heading East.

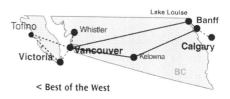

< Best of the West

Route and Trip Length

You will be following the Trans-Canada Highway (Highway 1) for about 1100 kilometers; the distance is not far but there is plenty of sightseeing to keep you busy. After spending a few days in Vancouver, head up the Trans-Canada to Kamloops, continuing on to Revelstoke and on through Glacier National Park and into Banff National Park. Follow Highway 1 into Calgary and spend a few days exploring the city before heading east or returning to Vancouver.

Highlights & Activities...

Indulge in the amazing diversity of Vancouver city, from pubs serving fresh microbrews to the tower on top of the town to totem poles in Stanley Park. Take a ferry to Vancouver Island where you can kayak with the whales, have a microbrew or two along the flower-lined streets of quaint Victoria or head up to Nanaimo for some serious backwoods hiking and R&R. Rent a mountain bike, horse, or canoe and go to town in the wilderness around Kamloops. Have a steaming cup of coffee before you head out onto Shuswap Lake, named for a local tribe. Then move on to Glacier National Park and go fishing in the clear, glacier-fed streams. Rock walls and rushing waterfalls await you in Yoho National Park, and you will find plenty of distractions from gourmet dinners to hot tubs to snowboarding lessons in Banff. Finish up in Calgary, a clean and friendly city with a vibrant culture on the edge of Canada's pristine Rocky Mountains.

How to See it...

Campervan Rental - from $49Cn/day, page 16 (Wicked Campers); Adventure Tours - from $150Cn, page 14 (Moose Travel Network, West Trek Tours); Coach Greyhound (pg 67).

Best of the East >

6) Best of the East – Toronto to Halifax

Starting in the most exciting city in Canada, this itinerary loops you from dazzling Toronto to rich and vibrant Montréal and back through some of the natural scenic wonders of the country, giving you a diverse taste of Canada and its many treasures. City kids and country folks alike will find plenty to enjoy in this east coast extravaganza, from festivals in city streets to frogs on forest pathways.

From Montréal (before returning to Toronto), you also can travel to the distinct maritime cultures of Nova Scotia and New Brunswick, an ocean and nature lover's dream. Villages await you along with one-road towns, plenty of fresh seafood, a thriving Celtic culture, pockets of French speakers and the most amazing tidal surges in the world. Or from Toronto, explore the major cities of the Northeast and head to Montréal, Boston and New York returning to Toronto.

Route and Trip Length

From Toronto hop on Highway 401 to Kingston, continuing on to Montréal for a few days before heading north on Highway 15 to visit Mont-Tremblant. Loop around to Ottawa and head up through Fort-Coulonge and on to Algonquin Park, spending a few days before returning to Toronto. To visit Nova Scotia, head to Halifax from Montréal via Quebec City and Fredericton, New Brunswick.

Highlights & Activities...

Enjoy accessible Toronto and explore the city easily, from iconic CN Tower to the Eaton Centre, packed with over 250 cute shops and a huge flock of Canadian geese- in mobile form. Taste a bit of the Old World as you walk the cobblestone streets of Montreal, then hit the clubs for a peep at tomorrow's music. Rip Mont-Tremblant in half with your snowboard, then indulge yourself with a room at the elegant Chateau Laurier in Ottawa. Walk across the second-longest covered bridge in Canada at Fort Coulonge, and explore the many rivers, forests, and lakes of Algonquin Park. Travel the legendary Cabot Trail on Cape Breton Island, Nova Scotia where the wild ocean waves crash against the mountainous terrain, and hit the beach.

How to See it...

Adventure Tours - from $299, page 62-63 (Moose Travel Network); Coach Megabus (pg 69), Greyhound (pg 67)

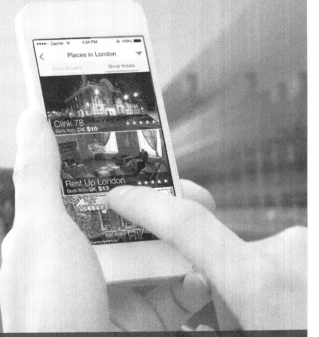

▸ backpacker tours

Arches National Park on a Trek America Tour

North America is chock-a-block with backpacker and independent traveler tours ranging from cool day trips to whopping 64-day mega adventures! A few companies operate tours all across North America including Trek America and Contiki, while others cover regional travel including the Southwest, Baja California (Mexico), Western Canada and Eastern Canada.

Hop-On, Hop-Off Passes
Also known as Jump-on/jump off tours, it's a great way to travel cheaply and at your own pace. While on the bus it's a tour and you have a guide that takes you around and can book local activities and accommodation. But you can get off at designated points along the way and catch the next bus coming through! Both Moose Network (Canada) and Screaming Eagle (Southwest) offer hop-on, hop-off passes. You can also stay on the bus the whole way if you are short on time, as if you were on a pre-set escorted tour.

Escorted Tours
In North America, these are mainly small group adventure tours in vans with up to 15-16 passengers. You travel with the driver/guide and a group of travelers for the entire pre-set itinerary.

Day Tours
Day tours are generally destination specific, like a city tour, pub crawl, adventure park or activity (surfing, hiking) or a visit to a breathtaking national or state park. Check your hostel reception and notice board for recommended tours.

Accommodation Options
Accommodation on tours varies but is generally hostels or camping. Some of the tour companies use budget hotels as well or some combination.

Departure Points
The most popular departure points are: New York, Los Angeles, San Francisco, Seattle and Miami in the US, and Vancouver and Toronto in Canada.

Seasonality
Many tours run year-round but the most options exist from May to October. Some companies, like Moose Network, only operate from May to October, while others have more limited options available during the off-season (Nov to April) and it will depend on where you are traveling.

Hop/Hop Off Tours
Moose Travel Network West
Western Canada (888) 244 6673
www.moosenetwork.com
10% Discount with code "Bakpak"
See their ad on page 62-63

Screaming Eagle Adventures
Southwest USA (888) 244 6673
www.screamingeagle.travel
10% Discount with code "Bakpak"
See their ad to the right

Adventure Tours
Contiki
USA/Can/Mexico www.contiki.com
Save $100 use code BakpakDave100
See their ad on page 9

Hostel Hiker
Baltimore/Wash DC (202) 670-6323
www.hostelhiker.com
See their ad on page 55

Moose Travel Network East
Eastern Canada www.moosenetwork.com
10% Discount with code "Bakpak"
See their ad on page 62-63

TrekAmerica
USA/Can/Mexico www.trekamerica.com
10% Discount with code "150260"
See their ads on page 1 and 41

West Trek Tours
Western Canada (604) 408-9378
www.westtrek.com
See their ad on page 61

1-3 Day Tours
A Day in LA Tours
Los Angeles www.adayinlatours.com
See their ad on page 32

Grand Canyon Hostel Tours
www.grandcanyonhostel.com
See their coupon on page 71

LA City Tours
Los Angeles www.lacitytours.com
See their ad on page 70

Shortline Tours
New York www.shortlinebus.com
See their ad on page 50

Southwest Adventures
Los Angeles www.sw-adventures.com
See their ad on page 32

➤ car/camper rentals

Hop in a car, get cozy in a campervan or take over the road in a camper or motorhome. There is no better way to see and experience America than the uber popular Road Trip! Gas is cheap compared to the rest of the world, roads are well maintained and easy to drive, and roadside amenities are excellent.

What are the Rental Requirements?
Generally you must be 21 years or older to rent a vehicle, although additional charges may apply for those under 25. A valid drivers license and major credit card is required but an international driver's license is not needed.

What are the costs involved?
The base rental rate, whether charged by day, week or month, is the most expensive part of the rental cost. Additional charges may be incurred for insurance, accessories like a GPS or for miles. Purchasing required miles is common for campers and motorhomes or you might pay for miles driven beyond those included in your base rate (commonly 100 miles per day).

What about car insurance?
There are two types of rental car insurance, Collision Damage Waiver (CDW), which covers damage to the vehicle itself and Supplemental Liability Insurance (SLI), which covers 3rd party claims for damage/injury to people or property. Some rental operators provide basic insurance in the base rental rate, some include all and some include no insurance, so be sure to check before signing an agreement. If not included, it will be listed as optional. You can check your car insurance policy back home to see if you are covered for car rental hire in the US or Canada.

What are Campervans (aka sleepervans)?
Campervans are converted mini-vans that have a table and seats in the back that convert to a full-size or queen size bed. They generally include a sink, mini-fridge, utensils, bedding, chairs and other equipment, but no toilet.

Campers and Motorhomes
These are the real deal. Roomier, more comfortable with toilets and full kitchens but also much more expensive. They can sleep between two and six travelers, thus making it affordable for a group of friends and backpackers.

Standard Pick Up/Drop Off Points
Available rental points for the companies listed here are New York, Los Angeles, San Francisco, Vancouver, Miami, Seattle, Denver and Las Vegas. The types of vehicles available at each location varies. Travel between locations is encouraged but there is a one-way fee applied, depending on the season and travel direction, and for cross-country rentals, a minimum one month rental period.

The following companies cater to backpackers and budget travelers including cross-country, one-way rentals. Pickup/drop-off points are listed below. For more info, see their ads which include phone numbers and websites.

Campervans
Escape Campervans
LA, San Fran, Vegas, New York, Miami
See their ad on page 19

JUCY
LA, San Fran, Vegas,
See their ad inside front cover

Lost Campers
LA, San Fran, Vegas,
See their ad on page 20

Adventures on Wheels
LA, San Fran, New York, Miami
See their ad on page 18

Wicked Campers
LA, Vancouver
See their ad on page 23

Campers/Motorhomes
Adventures on Wheels
LA, San Fran, NYC, Miami
See their ad on page 18

Apollo Motorhomes
LA, San Fran, Vegas, Denver
See their ad on page 21

Early Bird RV Rentals
Booking site for all US locations
See their ad on page 22

Cars and Minivans
Advanced Car Rental
Los Angeles. Ages 18 and older.
See their ad on page 22

Adventures on Wheels
LA, San Fran, New York, Miami
See their ad on page 18

Global All States Car Rental
Los Angeles
See their ad on pages 20 & 31

Super Cheap Car Rental
LA, San Fran, Orange County
See their ad to the right

Tell them Bakpak Dave sent you!

LOST CAMPERS

The best budget campervan company
on the West Coast of the USA

* Discreet modern vans
* San Francisco and LAX locations
* 24 hour roadside assist
* No youth fees - 21 or over
* Easy insurance options
* Camping and cooking equipment
* Fresh linens, Curtains, Comfy bed!

Call us:
+1 415 386 2693
free call within USA
1 888 lost van

reservations@lostcampersusa.com

www.lostcampersusa.com

$1 per night
Relocation Deals!

1-800-370-1262
www.apollorv.com

bakpak ▸▸ **united states**

The range of natural attractions, famed cities and cultural diversity on offer in the US means you'll have no shortage of places to visit and activities to pursue. Check out the forests, volcanoes, rivers and green cities of the Northwest; the sun, surf, Hollywood glam and bleak desert of the Southwest; the cultural activity and early American history of the Northwest; and the hospitality, beaches and tasty cuisine of America's South.

FEATURED HOSTELS & DESTINATIONS

The following destinations are excellent places to visit and each has one or more hostels in town so you can explore cheaply and meet other travelers.

Austin, Texas

Austin is known as the "Live Music Capital of the World," boasting over 100 venues offering a nightly range of music from blues to jazz. The happening part of town is 6th Street for nightlife but also check out the University of Texas campus and the capitol complex.

HI - Austin
2200 S. Lakeshore Blvd.
(512) 444-2294 (**❶** on map pg 6)
www.hiusa.org/austin
HI-Austin rests on the shores of Lady Bird Lake, providing a peaceful setting only minutes from downtown Austin. Our fun and friendly staff would love to give you ideas of what to do in town and directions to get there!

Waikiki, Hawaii

Waikiki Beach, on the island of Oahu, is one of the most popular backpacker destinations. Here, the nightlife and cheap eats are close by and open late. It's also the starting point for your adventures in Hawaii. There are tons of free and cheap activities to be found in and around Waikiki including the Arizona War Memorial, Diamond Head Crater, Punchbowl Crater and the Northshore. You can also try your hand at surfing, wind surfing, parasailing and of course body tanning.

Waikiki Beachside Hostel
2556 Lemon Road, Waikiki/Oahu
(808) 923-9566 (**❷** on map pg 6)
www.WaikikiBeachsideHostel.com
Rated the #1 hostel in Waikiki by Hawaiihostelsguide.com. Clean, safe, and secure accommodations only 1/2 block from Waikiki Beach. Toll free # 866-478-3888.

Newport, Rhode Is.

Newport, Rhode Island, is one of America's oldest cities, situated on an island midway between New York City, Boston, and Cape Cod, and is easily reached by public transportation. Newport is a walkable community with a treasure-trove of museums, historic buildings and rocky shoreline – all reminders of the city's past as a bustling colonial port and a 19th century millionaires' playground.

Newport Int'l Hostel
16 Howard Street
(401) 369-0243 (**❸** on map pg 7)
www.NewportHostel.com
Historic home in the heart of Colonial Newport's bustling waterfront and nightlife. Walk to beautiful beaches, historic mansions & Cliff Walk. Free parking nearby. Closed winter months (Jan-Mar). Beds from $25.

Buffalo/Niagara Falls, New York

Niagara Falls is only 22 miles from Buffalo. The falls separate the US and Canada, are over 180 ft tall, span over 3,000 feet and drop over 45 million gallons of water per minute.

Hostel Buffalo-Niagara
667 Main Street (**❹** on map pg 7)
(716) 852-5222
www.hostelbuffalo.com
A cozy & affordable homestead located in the heart of downtown, this non-profit hostel strives on accommodating travelers who come to explore the city and the falls.

Cape Cod, Massachusetts

Cape Cod, located 2 hours south of Boston, is a budget traveler's dream because of its great beaches and affordable lifestyle. Nantucket Island offers wildlife sanctuaries, reservations and parks. A great place to rediscover nature.

HI - Nantucket

31 Western Ave, Nantucket
(508) 228-0433 (⑤ on map pg 7)
www.hiusa.org/nantucket
The Nantucket hostel was built as a lifesaving station in 1873 and is listed on the National Register of Historic Places. It's also across the street from Surfside Beach and 3.5 miles from Nantucket village and ferry.

HI - Hyannis

111 Ocean Street, Hyannis
(508) 775-7990 (⑤ on map pg 7)
www.hiusa.org/hyannis
At HI-Hyannis, you don't have to go far to find the best the Cape has to offer - whether it's exploring Lewis Bay and Nantucket Sound by foot, kayak or windsurfer, hitting the beach or visiting local artist shanties.

Houston, Texas

Houston, aka "Space Town," aka "H-Town" is the largest city in Texas and fourth largest in the United States. Located along interstate 10, it's the next stop on your way west from New Orleans and home to a brand new hostel. Industries which have had a big influence here include oil and aerospace. Houston, "we have lift off..."

Tell them Bakpak Dave sent you!

HI - Houston, The Morty Rich Hostel

501 Lovett Boulevard
(713) 636-9776 (⑤ on map pg 7)
www.hiusa.org/houston
HI-Houston is located on a beautiful tree lined boulevard in the diverse and funky neighborhood of Montrose. We are within walking distance of some of the best bars, restaurants and coffee shops in Houston.

Los Angeles (LA) offers everything from beach life, to Hollywood fame to great nightclubs, eateries, live music venues and theme parks. And, you just can't beat the weather here! It's a great location to start your trip before moving on to the adventures of the west.

Where is LA

2 hrs north of San Diego on I-5, 6 hrs south of San Francisco on I-5, 5 hrs west of Las Vegas on I-15.

Coach, Rail & Tours

Greyhound (see ad page 5) two LA stations, downtown (1716 E 7th St) and Hollywood (1715 N Cahuenga Blvd). Travel to LA from San Francisco, San Diego and Las Vegas

Megabus (see ad page 34) travel to LA's Union Station from San Francisco or Las Vegas from $1.

Amtrak Union Station (800 N. Alameda St). Trains available from San Francisco and San Diego

Tours Trek America and Contiki offer tours that start and/or end in LA. See Backpacker Tours on page 14.

From the Airport

Public Transport shuttle "C" to the MTA Transfer Station for buses to Hollywood, Santa Monica, Venice Beach & downtown LA. Shuttle free, bus $1.50+

FlyAway Bus non-stop bus service between LAX and Westwood, Van Nuys or Union Station, $8-10 one-way (866-435-9529). For Hollywood, take Metro red line from Union Station to Hollywood and Highland stop.

SuperShuttle door-to-door shared ride service from $14+ (see their discount code on back cover)

Taxi about $30 to Venice, $40-60 to Santa Monica, $46.50 flat rate to downtown LA, $50+ to Hollywood

Getting Around

Big Blue Bus (Santa Monica, $1.00 , 310-451-5444)

MTA Buses (LA system wide, $1.50, 800-COMMUTE)

Dash Shuttle (Downtown LA, $.50, 213-808-2273)

Key Bus Routes Santa Monica to Hollywood (bus 534 to 780), Venice to Hollywood (bus 333 to 212)

Free Things to See & Do

Getty Museum free admission, parking $15 per car or take bus #761 from Santa Monica (310-440-7300)

Museum of Contemporary Art (MOCA) free Thurs, 5-8pm @ Grand & Geffen locations (213-626-6222)

Free TV show tapings On Camera Audiences (818- 295-2700), Audiences Unlimited (www.tvtickets.com)

Griffith Park featuring the LA Zoo, Griffith Observatory, hiking trails, outdoor concerts (323-913-4688)

Must See & Do

Venice Beach Boardwalk on weekends; **Bike Path** from Santa Monica to Hermosa Beach; Movie at Grauman's **Chinese Theater**; movie star homes and LA city tour; **Sunset Strip** in West Hollywood for nightlife; **Go hiking** in Griffith Park, Angeles National Forest, Topanga State Park or Will Rogers State Park; **Water Sports** learn to surf or stand up paddleboard.

Money Saving Tips

LA Stage Alliance half priced tickets (www.lastagetix.com)

LA Weekly pick up a copy free every Thursday for events, concerts and goings on

Farmers Markets buy fresh food around the City at various markets held weekdays and weekends

Day Tours

LA City Tours See their ad on page 70

A Day in LA Tours See their ad on page 32

Southwest Adventures 1-3 day tours to Joshua Tree, Yosemite and Death Valley. See their ad on page 32

Shopping Areas

Melrose Avenue, Farmer's Market/The Grove (West Hollywood); 3rd Street Promenade (Santa Monica); Fashion District b/w 8th & 9th Sts (Downtown LA); Rodeo Drive (Beverly Hills)

MOVING ON

San Diego plenty of hostels, great year-round climate, and relaxed, fun nightlife (pg 34)

Las Vegas what happens in Vegas, stays in Vegas. And don't you forget it (pg 39)

Baja California well worth the trip. Go past Tijuana for a real experience (pg 38)

San Francisco head north (pg 42)

California Coast heading north towards San Francisco (pg 33)

LOS ANGELES HOSTELS

Los Angeles hostels are mainly focused in three areas: Hollywood, Venice Beach and the Beaches south of LA (Hermosa/San Pedro). Due to traffic conditions and distances, it can take 30-60 minutes to travel between these locations. (see map on page 30 for locations/see page 70 for key to hostel icons)

Hermosa Beach

A happening surf suburb just 8 miles south of LAX. It boasts an excellent nightlife scene, miles of sandy beaches, great surf, and volleyball courts.

Los Angeles Surf City Hostel
26 Pier Avenue, Hermosa Beach
(310) 798-2323
www.SurfCityHostel.ws
See their ad next page

Hollywood

Hollywood Boulevard, Mann's Chinese Theatre, the Walk of fame plus plenty of bars/clubs and eateries.

Banana Bungalow Hollywood
5920 Hollywood Boulevard
(323) 469-2500
www.BananaBungalowUS.com
Hot Hollywood location! An "Oasis for Backpackers" with Free: internet, wireless, BBQ, breakfast, b-ball, billiards. Cable TV and kitchens in all dorms. This is the place to be.

See their ad on page 1 & 27

Orange Drive Hostel
1764 North Orange Drive
(323) 850-0350
www.orangedrivehostel.com
Best Kept Secret in Hollywood! 2 min. walk to major attractions, Chinese Theater, restaurants, clubs, shopping & more! Quiet Street in the middle of all the action!

See their ad on page 31

USA Hostels Hollywood
1624 Schrader Boulevard
(800) 524-6783
www.usahostels.com
See their ad on page 11

West Hollywood

Shopping/nightlife mecca. Melrose Ave., Sunset Strip bars, Grove and Farmers Market and CBS TV Studio.

Banana Bungalow West Hollywood
603 N. Fairfax Avenue
(323) 655-2002
www.BananaBungalowUS.com
Great location! Near Sunset Strip, Melrose, shopping, food, theaters, bars. Fun social hostel, lots of gatherings! Tiki courtyard & FREE: internet, wi-fi, breakfast, parking, activities & special access to Hollywood nightlife...

See their ad on page 1 & 27

LAX Area

Backpacker's Paradise
4200 West Century Boulevard
(310) 672-3090
www.backpackersparadise.com
Passport to Paradise. Imagine finding an air conditioned room with a tv, your bed made and room service. Everyday. All this for $15. Don't pass up your ticket to Paradise.

See their ad on page 31

Santa Monica

Beautiful beaches, Santa Monica Pier, hiking, biking, boardwalks and the latest in shopping. Check out Main Street or the pedestrian only Third Street Promenade.

HI - Santa Monica
1436 2nd Street
(310) 393-9913
www.hiusa.org/santamonica
Our purpose built hostel is located just two blocks from the beach in the heart of Santa Monica, a trendy tourist mecca and friendly seaside locale located west of downtown Los Angeles and just north of Venice.

See their ad on pages 36-37

San Pedro, South Bay

A seaside town in the South Bay, near Long Beach, Catalina Island and the many attractions of Orange county including Disneyland. (29 miles from LA).

HI-Los Angeles South Bay
3601 South Gaffey St #613, San Pedro
(310) 831-8109
www.hiusa.org/losangelessouthbay
Dramatic Ocean Views & Sunsets. Free parking and linen. Self-service kitchen & laundry. Free WiFi and Internet Access. No Curfew, Relaxed & Friendly. Open June 16-Sep. 8 2014.

Fullerton, Orange Co.

A charming town and birthplace of the Fender electric guitar, is located in Orange County close to Disneyland and Knotts Berry Farm (40 miles from LA).

HI-Fullerton (Los Angeles)
1700 North Harbor Blvd., Fullerton
(714) 738-3721
www.hiusa.org/losangelesfullerton
Closest Hostel to Disneyland! Free parking and linen. Kitchen, fireplace & laundry. Free WiFi and Satellite TV. No Curfew, Relaxed & Friendly. Open June 16-Sep. 8, 2014.

Tell them Bakpak Dave sent you!

SURF CITY HOSTEL

HERMOSA BEACH CALIFORNIA

W W W . S U R F C I T Y H O S T E L . C O M

26 Pier Ave Hermosa Beach CA

info@surfcityhostel.com

+1 (310) 798 2323

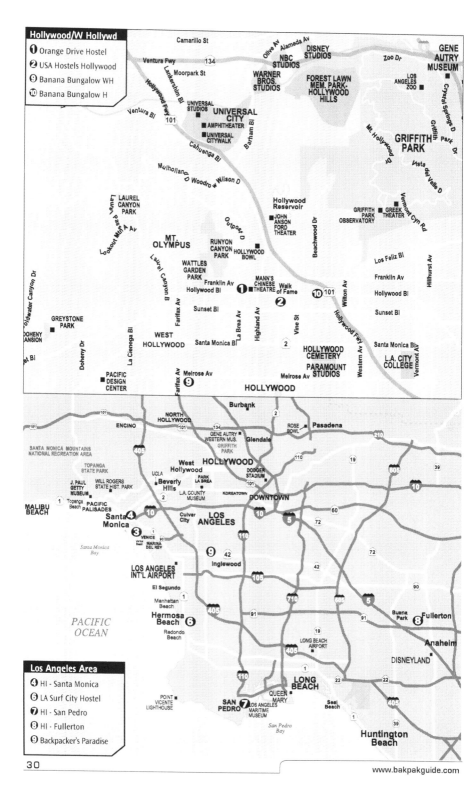

Hollywood/W Hollywd
- ❶ Orange Drive Hostel
- ❷ USA Hostels Hollywood
- ❾ Banana Bungalow WH
- ❿ Banana Bungalow H

Camarillo St
Olive Av   Alameda Av
NBC STUDIOS
DISNEY STUDIOS
Zoo Dr
GENE AUTRY MUSEUM
Ventura Fwy   134
Moorpark St
Lankershim Bl
Hollywood Fwy
WARNER BROS. STUDIOS
FOREST LAWN MEM. PARK- HOLLYWOOD HILLS
LOS ANGELES ZOO
Crystal Springs Dr
Ventura Bl
Ventura Fwy   101
UNIVERSAL STUDIOS
UNIVERSAL CITY
■ AMPHITHEATER
■ UNIVERSAL CITYWALK
Barham Bl
GRIFFITH PARK
Mt. Hollywood Dr
Griffith Park Dr
Cahuenga Bl
Mulholland D   Woodro W   Wilson D
Hollywood Reservoir
JOHN ANSON FORD THEATER
Beachwood Dr
GRIFFITH PARK OBSERVATORY
GREEK THEATER
Vermont Cyn Rd
Vista del Valle D
LAUREL CANYON PARK
Lookout Mtn A Av
Lookout Mtn Rd
MT. OLYMPUS
Laurel Canyon B
Outpost D
RUNYON CANYON PARK
HOLLYWOOD BOWL
Los Feliz Bl
Franklin Av
Hillhurst Av
Coldwater Canyon Dr
GREYSTONE PARK
WATTLES GARDEN PARK
Franklin Av
Hollywood Bl
❶ MANN'S CHINESE THEATRE
Walk of Fame
❷
❿ 101
Wilton Av
Franklin Av
Hollywood Bl
Sunset Bl
DOHENY MANSION
Doheny Dr
Sunset Bl
Santa Monica Bl
Fairfax Av
La Brea Av
Highland Av
Vine St
Sunset Bl
Hollywood Fwy
Western Av
Santa Monica Bl
L.A. CITY COLLEGE
Sel Bl
La Cienega Bl
WEST HOLLYWOOD
Santa Monica Bl
❷
HOLLYWOOD CEMETERY
Vermont Av
PACIFIC DESIGN CENTER
Fairfax Av
Melrose Av
❾
Melrose Av
PARAMOUNT STUDIOS
HOLLYWOOD

Burbank
101
NORTH HOLLYWOOD
101
134
ROSE BOWL
Pasadena
210
ENCINO
GENE AUTRY WESTERN MUS.
Glendale
SANTA MONICA MOUNTAINS NATIONAL RECREATION AREA
405
West Hollywood
HOLLYWOOD
GRIFFITH PARK
110
19
TOPANGA STATE PARK
UCLA
Beverly Hills
PARK LA BREA
DODGER STADIUM
805
39
J. PAUL GETTY MUSEUM
WILL ROGERS STATE HIST. PARK
101
L.A. COUNTY MUSEUM
KOREATOWN
DOWNTOWN
10
Topanga Beach
PACIFIC PALISADES
2
Culver City
LOS ANGELES
10
5
60
MALIBU BEACH
1
Santa Monica Bay
❹ 10
❸ 1
VENICE
MARINA DEL REY
110
72
PACIFIC OCEAN
❾ 42
Inglewood
42
72
LOS ANGELES INT'L AIRPORT
El Segundo
105
90
Manhattan Beach
1
710
405
5
Buena Park
❽ Fullerton
Hermosa Beach
❻
91
91
Anaheim
Redondo Beach
19
LONG BEACH AIRPORT
DISNEYLAND
405
22
22
405
LONG BEACH
POINT VICENTE LIGHTHOUSE
SAN PEDRO
❼ LOS ANGELES MARITIME MUSEUM
QUEEN MARY
Seal Beach
1
San Pedro Bay
39
Huntington Beach

Los Angeles Area
- ❹ HI - Santa Monica
- ❻ LA Surf City Hostel
- ❼ HI - San Pedro
- ❽ HI - Fullerton
- ❾ Backpacker's Paradise

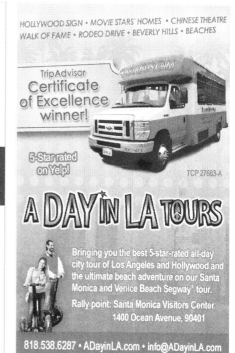

northern california & california coast ▶▶

CALIFORNIA COAST

The California Coast, also known as the Pacific Coast Highway (PCH 1 or Hwy 1) from Los Angeles to San Francisco features Santa Barbara, Big Sur, Hearst Castle, Monterey and Santa Cruz. The scenic beauty of the coast is on par with the most breathtaking in the world.

Highlights

Santa Barbara
A hip, rich town with golden beaches, museums and reasonably priced thrift stores/cafes. Check out State Street for trendy bars and clubs; the nearby mountains and valleys, for hiking and biking.

Hearst Castle
a sprawling estate of 165 rooms/127 acres of gardens, pools and walkways - book tours ahead! (800-444-4445).

Monterey/Carmel
known in the past for its huge fishing industry/sardine packing factories. Now, check out the world-class Monterey Bay Aquarium.

Big Sur
a spectacular 90-mile stretch of world famous coastline from San Simeon to Monterey (includes Pfeiffer Big Sur State Park/Big Sur River).

Montara and Pescadero
home to lighthouses converted to hostels. America's tallest lighthouse, Pigeon Point, stands at 115 feet and was built in 1872. Nearby are tide pools, redwood forests and gray whales. In season, you can see the whales, swim, surf and cycle along the shore.

Featured Hostels

HI - Pigeon Pt. Lighthouse
210 Pigeon Point Road, Pescadero
(650) 879-0633
www.hiusa.org/pescadero
Superb coastal setting with cozy rooms and ocean-side hot tub! Enjoy beaches, redwoods and whale-watching; hike, bike, kayak and visit elephant seals.

HI - Pt. Montara Lighthouse
16th Street & Hwy 1, Montara
(650) 728-7177
www.hiusa.org/montara
Extraordinary setting overlooking the Pacific. Cozy rooms, espresso bar, free WiFi. Enjoy beaches, tidepools, and whale-watching; hike, bike, surf, or kayak.

HI - Monterey
778 Hawthorne Street
(831) 649-0375
www.hiusa.org/monterey
Walk to Aquarium & beach, whale watching, kayaking, SCUBA diving, & surfing. Visit Carmel, Big Sur Coast, Steinbeck country. Free parking & pancake breakfast. Book reservations online.

NORTHERN CALIFORNIA

Northern California, from San Francisco to the Oregon border and inland towards Nevada, offers a wealth of natural beauty from pristine ocean shoreline, lakes, mountains and forests to vibrant smaller cities and towns. Check out places like Sacramento, Lake Tahoe, Wine Country, Yosemite National Park, Redwood National Forest and Point Reyes National Seashore.

Region Highlights

Sacramento
Located just 1.5 hours east of San Francisco and 1.5 hours west of Lake Tahoe the capital of California is steeped in Gold Rush history. This vibrant and cosmopolitan city offers friendly faces, a mild climate and a small town feel. Explore the many museums and wander through Old Sacramento, a key commercial and agricultural center during the 1940s.

Redwood National Park
Home of the old-growth coast redwoods. Some tower over 300 feet and are over 2000 years old! The park not only includes forest but rivers, streams and over 37 miles of ocean along the Northern California Coast. The park is located south of Klamath and entrance is free. Nearby is Jedediah Smith Redwoods State Park and Del Norte Coast Redwoods State Park which charge an entrance fee of just $6 per car.

Point Reyes
Further on up the coast you can go to Point Reyes Peninsula with its secluded beaches and miles of hiking trails.

Yosemite National Park
Located in the Sierra Nevada Mountains, Yosemite National Park was created in 1890 to preserve this amazing piece of nature that stretches from 2,000 to over 13,000 feet above sea level. Today it is one of the world's most impressive sceneries and home to the world-famous Half Dome and El Capitan. The park also boasts three giant sequoia groves, Tuolumne, Merced, and Mariposa. Many consider the giant sequoia trees the largest of all living things, some towering over 300 feet (91 meters) with tree trunks of 40 feet (12 meters) in diameter.

Featured Hostels

HI - Sacramento
925 H Street, Sacramento
(916) 443-1691
www.hiusa.org/sacramento
Experience the elegance of a Gold Rush mansion, along with modern comforts like free breakfast and WiFi. Walk to Capitol, historic sites, museums, and shopping.

HI - Point Reyes
Off Limantour Road, Point Reyes Nat'l Seashore. (415) 663-8811
www.hiusa.org/pointreyes
An eco-friendly hostel secluded in the Point Reyes National Seashore. Explore miles of trails through beaches and wetlands-- a bird-watchers paradise!

San Diego's climate averages 70°F (21°C) year round, which is reflected in the relaxed, laid-back nature of its residents. Due to San Diego's proximity to Mexico (gateway to Baja California) and early settlement history, a strong Spanish and Mexican influence exists.

Getting There

Car
2hrs south of Los Angeles off I-5

From Airport
(30-45 mins) MTS bus #992 for $2.25; Shuttle from $8; Taxis from $10

Coach & Rail
Greyhound (see their ad page 5) and Amtrak offer service from Los Angeles and other cities.

Getting Around
MTS bus and trolley system ($2.25 to $5, 619-238-0100)

Regional Day Passes 1 ($5), 2 ($9), 3 ($12), 4 ($15) days of unlimited rides on bus, ferry and trolley routes.

Things to See & Do

Free & Cheap
Timken Museum of Art in Balboa Park (619-239-5548); US Olympic Training Center (619-215-9070); Bernardo Winery, SoCal's oldest operating winery $10 for 5 wine tastings (858-487-1866); Museum of Contemporary Art, free at all 3 locations for 25 and under and 3rd Thurs of each month from 5-7pm (858-454-3541)

Money Saving Tips
Day Passes; Cabrillo National Monument/Pt Loma Lighthouse ($3 for 7 days, 619-557-5450); 3-attraction pass for Zoo/Wild Animal Park/Seaworld ($149, 619-231-1515); Science Center & 1 IMAX movie ($17, 619-238-1233); Balboa Park Passport Program, 14 museums for 1 week, $53, with Zoo, $89 (619-231-1640)

Must See & Do
Balboa Park; Coronado Island via ferry; San Diego Zoo; Pacific Beach nightlife; beaches; Baja California

Hostels
San Diego hostels are focused in downtown San Diego and the beachside suburbs of Pacific Beach and Ocean Beach. See map below for locations and page 70 for key to hostel icons.

California Dreams Hostel
743 Emerald Street, Pacific Beach
(858) 246-7101
www.californiadreamshostel.com
See their ad to the right

HI - San Diego Downtown
521 Market Street, Downtown
(619) 525-1531
www.hiusa.org/sandiegodowntown
Vibrant hostel in the heart of the Gaslamp Quarter. All dorm/private rooms have Tempur-Pedic© mattresses. Free breakfast and city tours.

HI - San Diego Point Loma
3790 Udall Street, near Ocean Beach
(619) 223-4778
www.hiusa.org/sandiegopointloma
Located in a friendly, quiet neighbor-hood, HI-San Diego Point Loma is just minutes from Ocean Beach. Recently voted #1 Specialty Lodging in San Diego on TripAdvisor.com, this hostel is a home away from home.

Lucky D's Hostel
615 8th Avenue, Downtown
(619) 595-0000
www.LuckyDsHostel.com
Best city location. Walk to all bars/clubs in the Gaslamp. Free Internet, waffle b/fast, pub crawl, tea/coffee, linen. Fun, friendly, social hostel. Dorms & privates rooms. Free dinner Tues, Thurs & Sunday!

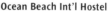

Ocean Beach Int'l Hostel
4961 Newport Avenue, Ocean Beach
(800) 339-7263
www.californiahostel.com
Have Fun, Sun, and Beach too. Free local transport to hostel. Central to Attractions/Mexico. Free Prepared breakfast daily. Free Barbecues Tues + Fri. Great hostel community here.

See their ad to the right

USA Hostels San Diego
726 5th Avenue, Downtown
(800) 438-8622
www.usahostels.com
See their ad on page 11

Greater San Diego
❶ HI San Diego Downtown
❷ USA Hostels San Diego
❸ Ocean Beach Hostel
❹ HI San Diego Pt Loma
❺ Lucky D's Hostel

STAY WITH FRIENDS
YOU'VE *NEVER* MET

Hostelling International USA hostels are as unique as the guests who stay with us. We're all about capturing the spirit of the community you're visiting, while making it easy to meet travelers from all over the world.

AUSTIN • BALTIMORE • BETHEL • BOSTON • CAMBRIA • CAPE VINCENT • CHICAGO •
HOUSTON • HYANNIS • KNOXVILLE • LOS ANGELES • LUCAS • MADISON • MERCED • M
PARK RAPIDS • PESCADERO • PHILADELPHIA • PHOENIX • POINT REYES • PORTLAND • O
SANTA CRUZ • SANTA MONICA • SAUSALITO • SEATTLE • SYRACUSE • TRURO • MARTHA'S V

HOSTELLING
INTERNATIONAL

baja california ▶▶

The long, skinny strip of land along the western edge of Mexico is known as Baja California. At the top lies Tijuana and the border between the United States and Mexico, while at the bottom rests the world-famous tourist, party-haven of Cabo San Lucas. In between is an always fascinating desert landscape of towering cactuses, sprawling beaches, secluded Mexican towns, and winding dirt roads (see page 70 for key to hostel icons).

Is it Safe?

The word from our Coyote Cal buddies is "One of the biggest questions on Northern Baja traveler's minds is safety. Over the last four years there have been many violent reports in the News. However, in the last year things have returned to normal. Big changes have been made in reforming the police departments and eliminating corruption and bribes. The police are professional and go out of their way to make tourists welcome. The war on drugs is also having success. The new Tijuana police chief has been very effective and violence that was once a daily event is now rare." You can check out their website, www.coyotecals.com for full details and loads of safety and travel tips.

Getting There

Car head south of San Diego and across the US border. It's 800 miles of arid peninsula from the border to Cabo San Lucas. Public Transport from San Diego, take the Blue Line/ Tijuana Trolley to San Ysidro and walk across the border (costs about $2.50, 40 mins) Coach ABC Bus Company (01-664-621-24-24) travels up and down Baja Cal from Tijuana to Cabo (29hrs). Baja Trek budget backpacking road trips and earth friendly camping adventures to beautiful beaches, mountains and deserts.

Baja California Highlights

Enseñada a couple of hours south of San Diego, along the coast is this popular party destination loaded with rowdy visitors and beaches. Make sure you try the fish taco. Beware though, this place is very touristy.

Tijuana is touristy and fun but it is not representative of the real Mexico and it's culture. You can get cheap drinks and food everywhere, but don't forget the health laws are a tad less stringent here and it is not the safest place to visit/stay at the moment.

Erendira is a small beach community about 60 miles south of Ensenada. Check with Coyote Cal's for the best directions and travel tips.

Points south A day's drive to Daggett's Camp at Bahia de Los Angeles puts you on the blue waters of the Sea of Cortes (no bus service, gas up in El Rosario). From January to March, see thousands of whales at Guerrero Negro or in the Mission town of San Ignacio.

Spending a day or two at EcoMondo on the Bahia Concepcion near Mulege and kayaking the tropical waters is a must. And the colonial town of Loreto is the place to learn of the history of Baja. If you want to avoid the big cities and tourist traps of La Paz and Cabo, stay at Pescadero surf camp a few miles south of Todos Santos. Also, Cerritos Beach offers warm waters and free camping.

Baja Hostels

Coyote Cal's Beach Resort
Erendira, Baja California
(011) 52-646-154-4080
www.coyotecals.com
See their ad to the left

Ensenada Backpacker
Segunda y Floresta 1429 Zona Centro, Ensenada
(011) 52 -646-177-1758
www.ensenadabackpacker.com

Tell them Bakpak Dave sent you!

las vegas

Las Vegas is world renown for its casinos and its gaudy super-lighted Strip, Las Vegas Blvd. Suffice to say, if you're looking to gamble, you're in the right spot. If you play your cards right, the least you should manage is a plentiful supply of free drinks and cheap eats like you've never seen before. But Vegas is not all about gambling - its got amusement parks, spectacular casino shows and a quite an amazing amount of natural beauty within a stone's throw of the city. You can get tours to Grand Canyon, Bryce Canyon, Zion National parks and Hoover dam from here too.

Getting There

Car
from Los Angeles 5hrs, San Francisco 10hrs, Zion 3hrs off I-15; from Flagstaff 4hrs off I-40/US93.

From the Airport
Public bus 108/109 for $3; Shuttle $6-8 o/w, $12-16 r/t; Taxi $20+ to downtown Vegas and the Strip.

Coach & Rail
Greyhound buses arrive from Los Angeles (7hrs), Flagstaff (5+hrs) and from San Fran (15hrs) (see their ad page 5). Megabus offers express service from Los Angeles and San Francisco (see their ad page 35)

Tours
Trek America offers a range of adventure tours that include Las Vegas on the itinerary as well as 3-4 day short-breaks from Los Angeles. Get 10% off their tours with discount code "150260." (see their ad on pages 1 and 41).

Screaming Eagle Bus Adventures offers hop off/off service in a route that includes Los Angeles, San Francisco and the Southwest. Get 10% off their tours/passes with discount code "Bakpak" (see their ad page 15).

Getting Around
CAT's Deuce on the Strip bus runs up and down the strip, 24hrs per day, every 15-20 minutes and costs $8 for a 24hr pass or $20 for a 3 day pass.

The Las Vegas Monorail stops at a majority of the strip/casinos and costs $5 per ride or $12 for a day pass.

Taxis operate 24/7 and can be a good way to get around but due to traffic can add up in price.

Casinos
Casinos in Vegas are everywhere. You can even lose your shirt at the slot machines without leaving the airport. With all the competition, the casinos have to try all sorts of strategies to draw crowds. So, in addition to the free drinks when gambling (even on the 5cent slots) and the cheap buffets, many casinos offer some form of theme park, hot night club or headline entertainment.

Things to See & Do

Free & Cheap
Bellagio Fountain show; Casino lounge shows; Ethel M Chocolate Factory & Botanical Cactus Gardens; Fremont Street Experience; Sirens of TI at Treasure Island; Exotic Cars at Caesars Palace; Lake of Dreams show at the Wynn; Water features at Aria Resort and Casino.

Money Saving Tips
Hit the buffets - try Circus Circus; pick up Showbiz magazine for coupons; free drinks when you gamble, even on penny and nickel slots.

Day Trips
Red Rock Canyon; Lake Mead and Hoover Dam; Lake Las Vegas; Bryce Canyon National Park, Zion National Park, Grand Canyon National Park (see page 40).

Hostels

Las Vegas Hostel
1322 Fremont Street
(800) 550-5958
www.lasvegashostel.net
See their ad below

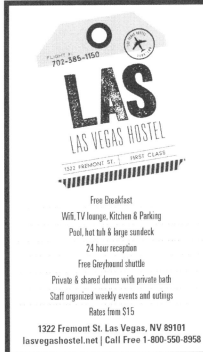

The Grand Canyon stands alone in the annals of canyons. There are deeper canyons, wider canyons and longer canyons, but none have the scintillating, spiral-colored majesty of the Grand Canyon. The Canyon is over a mile deep, 13 to 18 miles wide and 227 miles long. In addition to the Grand Canyon, the region, dubbed the "Grand Circle," includes Bryce Canyon, Zion National Park, Arches National Park, Canyonlands National Park, Lake Powell, Monument Valley, Mesa Verde and Capitol Reef.

Getting There

Car
Flagstaff, a jumping off location to the Grand Canyon with hostels is 8hr's from Los Angeles off I-40 from I-15; 2.5 hrs from Phoenix off 1-17; 5hrs west of Albuquerque, New Mexico.

Coach
Greyhound (399 S Malapais Lane, 928-774-4573) from Los Angeles, 12+hrs.

Tours
Grand Canyon Hostel Day trips to Grand Canyon for $85 (see their coupon page 71). Screaming Eagle Bus Adventures offers hop off/off service in a route that includes Los Angeles, San Francisco and the Southwest. Get 10% off their tours/passes with discount code "Bakpak" (see their ad page 15). Trek America (see their ad on page 1 and to the right) offer a range of hotel and camping based trips that visit the Grand Canyon region in small group adventure tour style.

Regional Highlights

Flagstaff
can be used as a base to explore the Grand Canyon region including Sedona and has two hostels and good nightlife scene due to the university.

Sedona
This popular spiritual town is 1hr or 30 miles due south from Flagstaff on US89. The drive to Sedona, through Pine Forest and Oak Creek Canyon, alone is worth the trip. Sedona IS red rock country and home to sacred vortexes. A must see destination if you are visiting Arizona.

Grand Canyon NP South Rim
The South rim is THE most popular destination inside the national park. The best way to see the Canyon is to hike it. Make sure you are well in-formed on the hazards. The desert is not forgiving, and make no mistake, the Grand Canyon is a desert. It will take twice as long to climb up as it did for you to descend. Most popular hike is the Bright Angel Trail.

Lodging can be booked a year ahead and the park campgrounds fill up fast. So check in nearby Tusayan. The South Rim is 90 miles north, on US 180, from Flagstaff. ($12pp or $25 per car, 928-638-7888).

Grand Canyon NP North Rim
The North Rim, at a higher elevation, is less traveled, but definitely worth the trip. At the North Rim, within walking distance of the Grand Canyon Lodge, is Bright Angel Point. It offers great views of the canyon (1/2 mile walk).The North Kaibab Trail leads to Roaring Springs (9.4 miles, 8 hrs r/t), a strenuous, all-day hike (take plenty of water). The North Rim is 220 miles by car from the South Rim. ($12pp or $25 per car, 928-638-7888)

Grand Canyon West Rim
This once lightly touristed corner of the Grand Canyon has been trans-formed into a big tourist attraction (or trap for some). The Grand Canyon Skywalk, a glass bridge that juts out from the canyon rim, 4000 feet above the Colorado River, costs $29.95+tax and you have to purchase the "en-trance fee" too which is $44.05. This includes a shuttle to Guano Point and the Hualapai Ranch (928-769-2636).

Zion National Park
An experience not to be missed. Trek through knee to waist high water, be-tween high cliff walls in the Narrows or check out the many monoliths - massive rock formations that extend up to 4,000 feet in the air. Or take a strenuous 14 mile hike to Kolob Arch,

one of the longest arches in the world. 41 miles from Kanab, Utah. ($12pp or $25 per car, 435-772-3256)

Bryce Canyon Nat'l Park
Filled with hoodoos - pillars of rock-like pinnacles and spires. Elevation exceeds 8,000 feet. Over 50 miles of hiking trails are available. Queen's Garden trail and Fairyland, Sunset, Farview, Yovimpa and Rainbow points all offer excellent views. Located off intersection of Rts 12 and 63 in Utah, 86 miles from Zion NP. ($12pp or $25 per car, 435-834-5322)

Canyonlands Nat'l Park
largest of Utah's parks is set in a desert climate. Probably the most untouched of the parks, thereby retaining its unique ruggedness. Rent bikes in Moab. ($5pp or $10 per car, 435-719-2313)

Arches Nat'l Park
Over 2,000 arches ranging in size from 3 feet to over 300. Water, ice and extreme tem-peratures over the last 100 million years led to these formations. Located off Hwy 191 in Utah, 5 miles northwest of Moab. ($5pp or $10 per car, 435-719-2299)

Flagstaff Hostels

Grand Canyon Int'l Hostel
19 S. San Francisco
(928) 779-9421
www.grandcanyonhostel.com
Welcome! Super clean, fun, friendly, safe! FREE, tasty breakfast, FREE WiFi. Awesome tours to Grand Canyon and Sedona. Call us toll-free 1-888-442-2696.

See their ad to the right

Motel DuBeau Inn & Hostel
19 West Phoenix Avenue
(928) 774-6731
www.modubeau.com
See their ad to the right

Flagstaff Hostels

Award Winning Locations in Historic Downtown Flagstaff—gateway to the Grand Canyon!

Discounted Grand Canyon Hiking Tours; see our coupon in back

Grand Canyon International Hostel

Welcoming happy travelers for over 20 years!

Charming, Cozy, Friendly, Affordable

"Nature Inspired" PRIVATES / 4 person DORMS

1.928.779.9421 / 1.888.44CANYON

www.grandcanyonhostel.com

M🌎tel DuBeau Travelers Inn and Hostel

An Original Route 66 landmark, Lovingly restored, Artisan inspired!

Quaint Privates / Dormitory Suites

Coming soon to the "Mo"... **NOMADS**; a vintage lounge

"Where the World comes to Mingle"

1.928.774.6731 / 1.800.398.7112

www.modubeau.com

San Francisco is one of the most beautiful cities in the world. It's a place to see by foot. Gotta love those wicked hills! There are so many interesting areas and sites, with great views of the bay and city that are free, you can save your money for food and drink.

Where is San Francisco
6hrs north of Los Angeles off I-580 from I-5, 15hrs south of Seattle, 10.5hrs west of Salt Lake City

Coach & Tours
Greyhound Transbay Terminal (425 Mission Street, 415-495-1569). Buses arrive from Los Angeles (8-12hrs), Seattle (23+hrs) and Salt Lake City (15.5hrs)

Megabus coach buses arrive from Los Angeles and Sacramento at the Caltrans Station at 700 4th Street.

Screaming Eagle hop-on/off passes that can start/end in San Francisco. See their ad on page 15.

From the Airport
Public Transport SFO, Air Train from terminals to BART Yellow/Red line ($8.65, get off at Civic Center/ Powell or Montgomery stops for most hostels/hotels); From Oakland Airport, take AirBart to BART to stops listed above in San Francisco ($4.05).

SuperShuttle from $15 (see discount on back cover)

Taxi $35-40 to downtown

Getting Around
BART (415-989-2278) underground rail lines that serve the city and East Bay (Berkeley/Oakland). Cost per trip is based on distance traveled

San Francisco MUNI (Dial 311) buses & streetcars ($2), cable cars ($6/each way, $15 for a 1-day pass), best way to get around the city, MUNI Passport for unlimited rides including cable cars: 1-day ($15), 3-day ($23) or 7-day ($29)

Free Things to See & Do
Walk down Lombard Street (crooked street, start at top of the hill at Hyde Street)

Yuerba Buena Gardens contained within Mission, Folsom, Third and Fourth Streets in the SOMA district

Presidio explore the Presidio with the free PresidiGo Park Shuttle. Take MUNI bus #28, 29, 43 or 82X from Union Square area to the Presidio gate

Coit Tower at the top of Telegraph Hill ($7 to top)

San Francisco Art Institute (800 Chestnut St)

Must See & Do
Explore all the great neighborhoods; walk/bike across Golden gate Bridge; Alcatraz Tour from Pier 41 (book in advance during summer); take the 49-mile Scenic Drive; Cable car ride; Coit Tower during day and on a clear night; Twin Peaks for great city views; check out the Seals hanging out at Pier 39; Sample the seafood from street side stalls at Fisherman's Village.

Money Saving Tips
Buy a MUNI-pass 1-7 days or a 1-day Cable Car pass

Look for coupons in free city guides for discounts to many touristy and not so touristy attractions

Neighborhoods
Mission District; Haight-Ashbury; Chinatown/North Beach; Castro; Golden Gate Park; SOMA for nightlife; Berkeley; Sausalito

Shopping Areas
Union square; Haight-Ashbury; Chinatown

Day Trips
Napa/Sonoma wine country (2hrs); Big Sur (2.5hrs); Stinson Beach/Muir Woods (just over Golden Gate Bridge); Yosemite National Park (4hrs).

Hostels
Adelaide Hostel
5 Isadora Duncan Lane
(877) 359-1915
www.adelaidehostel.com
See their ad to the right

HI - SF Downtown Hostel
312 Mason Street
(415) 788-5604
www.hiusa.org/sanfranciscodowntown
Just one block from Union Square, steps from cable cars and Chinatown. FREE breakfast, WiFi, wine tasting, pub crawls, walking tours, and more. Newly remodeled. Only 4 beds per dorm; private rooms available.

HI - Marin Headlands Hostel
Fort Barry Bldg 941, Sausalito
(415) 331-2777
www.hiusa.org/sausalito
A convenient alternative base for visiting San Francisco, just 5 miles from the Golden Gate Bridge in a spectacular coastal National Park.

The Adelaide Hostel

5 ISADORA DUNCAN LANE, SAN FRANCISCO, CA
1-877-359-1915 - WWW.ADELAIDEHOSTEL.COM

The best free breakfast in San Francisco!
24 hour reception, free bike & luggage storage!
Free computers & Wifi!
Events 7 Nights a week!
Free meals 2 nights a week!
Discounts on Tours, Bike Rentals, & More!

Come see San Francisco!

HI - SF City Center Hostel
685 Ellis Street
(415) 474-5721
www.hiusa.org/sanfranciscocitycenter
Beautifully renovated 1920s boutique hotel. 4-bed dorms and private rooms, each with ensuite bath. Café serving beer and wine nightly. FREE breakfast, WiFi, pub crawls, walking tours. Central location near sights and transit.

**HI - SF Fisherman's
Wharf Hostel**
Fort Mason, Bldg. 240,
Bay & Franklin
(415) 771-7277
www.hiusa.org/sanfranciscowharf
Historic hostel in a National Park with views of Alcatraz/Golden Gate Bridge. FREE breakfast, WiFi, parking. On-site cafe, free activities daily, Napa/ Yosemite tours. Near North Beach, Fisherman's Wharf, Pier 39, cable cars

USA Hostels San Francisco
711 Post Street
(877) 483-2950
www.usahostels.com
See their ad on page 11

Portland, 3 hours south of Seattle, has been called America's most European city. It is known for its friendly people, its strong music scene, and its connection to nature in and around the city.

Getting There

Car
14hrs from San Francisco and 3hrs from Seattle on I-5.

From the Airport
TriMet Light Rail Red Line every 5-15 mins from 5am to 11:49pm. Costs $2.50 and takes about 38 mins.

Coach & Rail
Greyhound (550 NW Sixth Ave, 503-243-2361). Buses arrive from San Francisco (16+hrs) and Seattle (4+hrs).

Amtrak (800 NW 6th Ave) The Coast Starlight operates from Los Angeles to Seattle via Portland. From San Francisco it is 18hrs, from Seattle (3.5hrs).

Getting Around
TriMet bus, MAX Light Rail or Portland Street Cars are free all day, everyday in the Portland City Center, Rose Square and the Lloyd District (Fareless Square). Otherwise 2hr tickets cost $2.50, All-Day $5, weekly $26.

Things to See & Do
No shopping sales tax; Int'l Rose Test Garden (free, bus #63); Portland Attractions Pass - 4 pass types from $19-55, valid for 5 days; walk Portland's streets, voted one of America's Best Walking Towns; Portland buses, light rail trains & street-cars are free in Portland's "Fareless Square" district; Open air markets, the downtown river loop, micro brewery tours.

Portland Hostels

HI - Portland, Northwest
425 NW 18th Avenue
(503) 241-2783
www.nwportlandhostel.com
See their ad below

HI - Portland Hawthorne
3031 SE Hawthorne Boulevard
(503) 236-3380
www.hiusa.org/portlandhawthorne
Portland's original hostel, located in the bohemian Hawthorne District of Southeast Portland. Hawthorne Blvd is known for it's quaint eateries, coffeehouses, pubs, unique shops, and the famous Bagdad Brewpub & Theatre.

**Tell them Bakpak
Dave sent you!**

boston

Boston, known as Beantown, is a huge college town, a crazy place to drive, and steeped in Irish heritage. Laze around on Boston Commons in the middle of the city; this historic green space is now full of students, not livestock. Slurp New England clam chowder as you watch the seals come in with the tide or visit one of the best aquariums in the States.

Getting There

Car
3.5hrs north of New York City on I-95; 10 hrs south east of Toronto; 6 hrs south of Montreal; 18.5 hours east of Chicago.

Coach & Rail Stations
Greyhound South Station (700 Atlantic Ave, 617-526-1801). Buses arrive from New York (4.5hrs), Montreal (7hrs) and Philly (7hrs)

Megabus offers Wifi enabled coach buses to Boston's South Station (700 Atlantic Ave, megabus.com) from New York ($1+, 4.5hrs)

Amtrak Back Bay (145 Dartmouth St), South Station (Summer & Atlantic), catch the "T" from South Station or Back Bay Station to points in Boston

From the Airport
Public Transport free shuttle bus (#22 or #33) from the airport to the Airport Blue line T stop ($2, to the city). **Water Taxi** $10 boats you across the bay, catch the free #66 bus from the terminal.

Getting Around
The "T" ($2, 617-222-3200) Boston's four color-coded line subway system (red, green, orange and blue). Get a LinkPass $11 (1-day), $18 (7-day) unlimited travel on T and buses.

Things to See & Do

Free & Cheap
Museum of Fine Arts (465 Huntington Ave) voluntary donation every Wednesday after 4pm. Japanese Gardens behind museum free admission everyday (closed winters).

Freedom Trail Boston's most famous self-guided walking tour stretches 2.5-miles/4-km, starts at 15 State Street opposite the Old State House.

Institute of Contemporary Art free Thurs 5-9pm (955 Boylston St).

Irish Heritage Trail 3 hour self-guided walking tour. Starts at Rose Kennedy Garden along the waterfront (free maps at Boston Commons visitor booth).

USS Constitution Tours free guided tours from the US Navy of the oldest US warship, from 1797 (1 Constitution Road, Charlestown Naval Yard).

Must See & Do
Harvard Square; Freedom Trail; Whale Watching Cruise; Quincy Market; New England Aquarium.

Money Saving Tips
College 'hoods for cheap party places including Boston University, Boston College, MIT and Harvard.

Bostix half price, day of show theater tickets with locations in Copley Square and Faneuil Hall.

Neighborhoods
The North End (authentic Italian, Hanover St); Boston Common (contains 48-acres of public park located in the center of Boston); Back Bay offers many restaurants and pubs; Cambridge wander around Harvard, the nation's first university, and Harvard Square.

Shopping Areas
Newbury/Boylston Street (Back Bay); Filene's Basement (Downtown Crossing); Faneuil Hall Market place; Harvard Square.

Hostels

40 Berkeley
40 Berkeley Street
(617) 375-2524
www.40berkeley.com
See their ad below

HI - Boston
19 Stuart St
(617) 536-9455
www.hiusa.org/boston
HI-Boston is in the Chinatown / Theater District area, which includes some of the best entertainment the city has to offer. In a few short minutes you can walk around to Boston Common and get to the famous Freedom Trail.

philadelphia ▶▶

Philadelphia is the original capital of the United States, where the declaration of independence was signed in 1776. The "City of Brotherly Love," located between New York City and Washington, DC, boasts a great nightlife, many historical landmarks and was recently rated the 3rd most walkable city in the country after New York and San Francisco. Don't leave without trying a Philly cheese steak sandwich - the rumors are true indeed.

Getting There

Car
2hrs south of New York off I-95

Coach
Greyhound downtown Station (1001 Filbert St. 215-931-4075). Buses arrive from New York (2hrs) and Washington DC (4-6hrs).

Megabus offers Wifi enabled coach buses downtown bus Stop (600 Market St.) from New York ($1+, 2hrs), from Washington DC ($1+, 3hrs).

Rail
Amtrak 30th Street Station (30th and Market, 1-800-872-7245) trains arrives from New York City (1.5hrs) and Washington DC (2hrs).

From the Airport
Public transport SEPTA R1 train to Market East Station downtown ($6.50+). Shuttle Liberty Shuttle to downtown ($10+). Taxi to downtown ($28.50 flat rate).

Getting Around
SEPTA operates Philadelphia's buses, trolleys and subways. Fares are $2.25 and require exact change (tokens are $1.80). A One Day Convenience Pass costs $8 and is valid for up to eight bus, trolley or subway trips.

Things to See & Do
Free & Cheap
Philadelphia Museum of Art featuring steps from the movie "Rocky" (215-763-8100, 26th St. and B. Franklin Pkwy) pay what you wish 1st Sunday of month.

Independence Hall free guided tour tickets available at Visitors Center (215-965-2305, 600 Chestnut St.)

US Mint free tours M-F (215-408-0209, 151 N. Independence Mall E)

Rodin Museum pay what you wish. (215-568-6026, 2151 Benjamin Franklin Pkwy).

Must See & Do
Eastern State Penitentiary world's first penitentiary features former cell of Al Capone (215-236-3300, 2124 Fairmount Ave.); South Street (between 1st and 10th Streets) popular stores bars and restaurants; Mosaic Garden (1020 South Street); Elfreths Alley oldest inhabited street in the USA (2nd Street between Arch and Race Streets); Liberty Bell 215-965-2305 (526 Chestnut St.); Betsy Ross House she sewed the first American flag; Benjamin Franklin's grave (Christ Church Burial Ground, corner of 5th and Arch).

Neighborhoods
Old City (historical area/great nightlife); Society Hill; Gayborhood; Chinatown; Parkway/Museum District; Rittenhouse Square (shopping); University City.

Hostels

Apple Hostels of Philadelphia
32 S. Bank Street
1-877-275-1971
www.applehostels.com
Rated as one of the top 3 hostels in USA by Hostelworld. Steps from Independence Hall, Liberty Bell, pubs, restaurants and nightclubs. Free Wine and Cheese Movie Nights on Tuesdays. ISIC cards honoured.

See their ad to the right

Chamounix Mansion International Hostel
3250 Chamounix Dr, W Fairmount Park
(215) 878-3676
www.philahostel.org
Historic mansion in park. Bike and hiking trails at doorstep. Minutes to city's culture and arts; river sports and events. Free parking, bikes and wi-fi Full kitchen, laundry, lockers.

applehostels

Among top 5 hostels in America 5 years in a row*

free
WiFi
Coffee & tea
Drinks every night
Wednesday pasta dinners
Thursday pub crawls
Friday wine & cheese
Nintendo Wii

we know **Philadelphia.**

- NO curfews or lockouts
- Central air-conditioning
- Fully equipped kitchen
- Onsite laundry facilities
- 24-hour reception
- $2 ghost tours
- Downtown's only hostel

know **where** you've been.

CALL: 1-877-275-1971
www.applehostels.com
32 S Bank St, Philadelphia

*according to Hostelworld customers
minimum 300 reviews

new york city

Ah, New York, New York. So good, they named it... well, you know the rest. There is so much to see and do here. It's best to let you explore the most amazing city in the world! Every turn of the corner will provide an opportunity to experience the new, exciting or unexpected.

Where is New York
3.5hrs south of Boston, 4.5hrs north of Washington DC, and 2hrs north of Philadelphia on I-95; 9 hrs from Toronto; 7 hrs from Montreal; 15hrs from Chicago.

Coach, Rail & Tours
Greyhound Port Authority Bus Terminal (8th Ave & 42nd, 212-971-6300). Buses arrive from Boston (5hrs), DC (4.5hrs), Toronto (11hrs) and Chicago (18hrs).

Megabus (www.megabus.com) fares from $1 on coach buses with free Wifi. Station next to Penn Station (31st/8th Ave.) from Boston ($1+, 4.5hrs), Philly ($1+, 2hrs), Wash. DC ($1+, 4.5hrs), Toronto ($1+, 10hrs).

Amtrak Penn Station (33rd & 8th Ave, 212-630-6400).

Shortline Bus offers day trips to the Woodbury Commons Outlet, Bear Mountain and the beautiful Hudson Valley (see their ad on page 50).

From the Airport
Public Transport JFK (AirTrain from terminals to the A train to City, $7.50); LaGuardia (M60 bus to 106th St/Broadway, $2.50, connect with free transfer to other bus/subway lines); Newark ($15 total, AirTrain to NJ Transit train station to Penn Station, Manhattan).

Shuttle SuperShuttle (from JFK/LaGuardia, $23/$15, (see discount on back page); Newark Liberty Airport Express (to Grand Central Station, $16 o/w, $28 r/t, (see their ad and coupon on page 52).

Taxi from JFK flat $52+toll/tip to Manhattan; LGA about $25+tip; Newark is meter+$15+toll/tip ($50+).

Getting Around
MTA (718-330-1234) subway, buses , LIRR and Metro North. Subways and buses operate 24hrs. Always buy a Metrocard to get around (by trip $2.50, weekly $30) as transfers from bus-bus & subway to bus are free.

Free Things to See & Do
Museum of Modern Art free Fridays 4-8pm (11 W 53rd St).

New York Botanical Gardens free Wednesday all day & 10am-11am Sat (Bronx, 718-817-8700).

Staten Island Ferry free (Battery Park terminal).

Central Park stretches from 59th St to 110th St, between Central Park West and Fifth Ave.

Must See & Do
Empire State Building; Statue of Liberty; Village; Harlem; eat a bagel w/cream cheese; eat a hot dog in Central Park; Chinatown & Little Italy; Circle Line Tour (see their ad on page 51).

Money Saving Tips
TKTS (Father Duffy Square, B'way & 47th Street) half price, same day theater tickets for evening shows (3pm-8pm) and or matinees on Wed and Sat (10am-2pm).

Bronx Zoo pay as you wish on Weds (718-367-1010).

Pick up copy of the free Village Voice every Thursday for events, concerts and goings on.

Neighborhoods
Chinatown; East & West Village; SOHO; Lower East Side; Upper West Side; Times Square; Hell's Kitchen.

Shopping Areas
Canal Street (Chinatown); West Village (8th St b/w 6th/3rd Aves); SOHO (Broadway from 8th St to W Houston St).

Day Trips
Take the Shortline Bus to the famous Woodbury Commons Outlets (see their ad on page 59); Woodstock (2.5hrs); Spend a day exploring the NYC boroughs - Queens, Bronx, Brooklyn, Staten Island.

International Student Center

A Cozy Youth Hostel in New York City

- Located on the Upper West Side of Manhattan...steps away from Central Park
- Close to B and C, 1 and 9 Subway trains
- Dormitory style accommodation for travelers ages 18-35
- Full kitchen facilities, INTERNET PC, lounge with TV
- Secure storage area and locked safe for your belongings
- Friendly, international staff
- Beautiful summer garden...with free fresh herbs for you to cook!
- Ongoing programs...FILM FORUM/POETRY/ART SHOWS
- Our Musician in Residence Program offers: music sessions & singer, song writer workshops

38 West 88th Street, NY, NY 10024 (212) 787-7706 (8am-11pm)
info@nystudentcenter.org   www.nystudentcenter.org

dorms from $30

Hostels

HI - New York
891 Amsterdam Ave., Upper West Side
(212) 932-2300
www.hiusa.org/nyc
The world's greatest hostel, in the very heart of the world's greatest city. It's where adventurers from around the world gather to share ideas and experiences while visiting New York City.

See their ad on pages 36-37

International Student Center
38 West 88th Street, Upper West Side
(212) 787-7706
www.nystudentcenter.org
See their ad on page on page 49

Vanderbilt YMCA
224 East 47th Street, Midtown
(212) 912-2500
www.ymcanyc.org/reservations
See their ad to the right

West Side YMCA
5 West 63rd Street, Upper West Side
(212) 912-2600
www.ymcanyc.org/reservations
See their ad to the right

BE IN THE CENTER OF ALL THE ACTION

the **Y** YMCA®

FOR YOUTH DEVELOPMENT
FOR HEALTHY LIVING
FOR SOCIAL RESPONSIBILITY

STAY AT A NEW YORK YMCA!

The YMCA offers the best locations in New York City. You can have **pools**, **gyms**, **air conditioners** and **cable TV** at affordable prices.

Harlem YMCA - Heart of Harlem
180 West 135th Street
New York, NY 10030
212-281-4100

Vanderbilt YMCA - Near United Nations
224 East 47th Street
New York, NY 10017
212-912-2500

West Side YMCA - Steps from Central Park
5 West 63rd Street
New York, NY 10023
212-912-2600

Greenpoint YMCA - Brooklyn
99 Meserole Avenue
Brooklyn, NY 11222
718-389-3700

Flushing YMCA - Queens
138-46 Northern Boulevard
Flushing, NY 11354
718-961-6880 x133

For Reservations
call (917) 441-8800 or go to
www.ymcanyc.org/guestrooms

baltimore/wash. dc ▶▶

These three cities are a must stop on your USA backpacking trip. Each offer tons of free and cheap things to see and do and are easy to get to and from with a $1+ Megabus.com fare!

BALTIMORE

Baltimore offers a relatively new hostel located in the heart of downtown, where you can explore the waterfront harbor, hop on a water taxi, visit the aquarium and shop at the world famous Lexington Market.

Getting There

Greyhound (2110 Haines St, 410-752-0919), from New York (4+ hours); **Megabus** travel by luxury coach with free Wifi (White Marsh Park & Ride, www.megabus.com) from New York ($1+, 3.5 hours).

HostelHiker offers scheduled transport directly between hostels in Baltimore, Washington DC and Harpers Ferry (see their ad below).

From the Airport

Take **MTA** Bus 17 or the Light Rail to downtown for $1.60. Taxi costs $35+ to downtown. **SuperShuttle** door to door service from $13 (get 10% off with their code on the back cover).

Getting Around

The new Charm City Circulator is free and offer three shuttle routes and a water taxi in and around Baltimore City.

Baltimore Hostels

HI - Baltimore
17 West Mulberry Street
(410) 576-8880
www.hiusa.org/baltimore
Brownstone mansion in Downtown Baltimore. Walking distance to Inner Harbor, brew pubs, sports stadiums, and nightlife. Dorm style & private rooms. Free pancake breakfast, WiFi. Reception open 24 hrs.

Things to See & Do

Baltimore Heritage Walk discover historic Baltimore with this $7 walking tour of 20 historic sites/museums. (Apr-Nov, 410-878-6411)

Walters Art Museum over 25,000 pieces of art. Free. (600 N. Charles St)

Fell's Point's cobble stoned streets border the waterfront and are filled with theaters, cafes, art galleries, parks, museums and free movies.

WASHINGTON DC

Washington DC is home of the nation's capitol, the Smithsonian Museum and some of the best historic monuments. In contrast to staid politics, it is also a young town with lots of cool bars.

Getting There

Coach & Rail
Greyhound (1st and L Sts), from New York (4.5 hours); **Megabus** (G St NW & 9th St NW, www.megabus.com) from New York ($4+, 4.5 hours).

HostelHiker offers scheduled transport directly between hostels in Baltimore, Washington DC and Harpers Ferry (see their ad to right).

Things to See & Do

Government
White House tours (15th and E Sts NW, get there early); Bureau of Engraving & Printing (U.S. Treasury Dept. at 14th & C Sts SW); Observe the Supreme Court in session (1st St NW & E Capital St); Tour the Pentagon (Arlington, VA).

Museums
Holocaust Museum (100 Raoul Wallen-berg Place SW); The Smithsonian Museums

(the National Mall); Nat'l Air & Space Museum (Indep. Ave. & 7th St., SW).

Memorials
Jefferson Memorial (900 Ohio Drive SW); Tomb of the Unknowns (Arlington Nat'l Cemetery); Lincoln Memorial (900 Ohio Dr. SW); Vietnam Vets Memorial (Constitution Ave. and Henry Bacon Dr. NW).

HI - Washington, DC
1009 11th Street, NW
(202) 737-2333
www.hiusa.org/washingtondc
Located near the city's most famous attractions, HI-DC offers a friendly and inexpensive lodging experience. We provide an unbeatable environment and a long list of amenities & many are FREE.

chicago ▶▶

Chicago has been aptly dubbed the "Windy City" due to the strong gusts coming from Lake Michigan. Not only does Chicago have the most outdoor sculptures made by world-famous artists, and excellent lakefront beaches in the city, it is the home of the famous "deep-dish" pizza.

Getting There

Car
In the heart of the Midwest, 15 hrs from New York off I-80, 5hrs from Detroit off I-94, 10hrs from Toronto off Hwy 401 & I-94, 35hrs from San Fran.

Coach & Rail
Megabus Union Station, Chicago to/from a host of Midwest cities (www.megabus.com) See ad page 51.

Greyhound 630 West Harrison St (312-408-5821), from New York (17+hrs), Toronto (11.5hrs), San Francisco (51hrs)

Amtrak 225 South Canal St, New York (19hrs), Toronto (11.5+hrs), San Fran (55hrs).

From the Airport
Public Transport from O'Hare take blue Line to downtown, $2.25/$.25 for transfer. **Shuttle** $27. **Taxi** $40-45 to downtown; ask for shared ride $22/person.

Getting Around
Chicago Transit Authority (CTA) buses and trains including the famous "L" aboveground line. $2.25 cash or prepaid card; unlimited day passes 1-day ($10), 3-day ($20), 7-day ($28).

Things to See & Do

Free & Cheap
Chicago Cultural Center free public events including music, dance and film (78 E. Washington St.)

The Second City free improv set follows the last performance every night except Friday (1616 N Wells St)

Lincoln Park Zoo One of the oldest Zoos in the US, it includes 35-acres of awesome animals including gorillas (2001 N Clark St)

Museum of Contemporary Photography (600 S Michigan Ave)

Navy Pier located on Lake Michigan, the Pier offers 50 acres of parks, promenades, gardens, shops, restaurants and rides. Boat cruises also available from here

Millennium Park in the heart of the city of Chicago with cultural events, gardens, and an ice rink. Bicycle parking available here.

Must See & Do
Sears Tower observation desk; Lake Michigan beaches along Lake Shore Drive; Wrigley Field for Cubs baseball game; Lincoln Park Zoo.

Neighborhoods
Hyde Park; South Shore; Ukrainian Village; Uptown; Pullman Historic District; Chinatown; Wicker Park; Wrigleyville; Lincoln Park.

Tours
Take a Hop On Hop Off Tour, a 2-hour tour which gives you transportation to the most famous Chicago attractions, covering 13 magnificent miles of Chicago's downtown and the Loop.

Hostels

Getaway Hostel
616 W. Arlington Place
(773) 929-5380
www.getawayhostel.com
Located in a trendy university area of Lincoln Park with dozens of bars, clubs, pubs and music venues. Walking distance to North Avenue Beach, Lincoln Park Zoo, biking/running trails, public transport.

See their ad to the right

HI - Chicago
24 E. Congress Parkway
(312) 360-0300
www.hiusa.org/chicago
Located in the center of the city, HI-Chicago is a 500-bed hostel offering guests safe, clean, quality accommodations near major attractions and public transportation.

miami beach ▶▶

Miami offers everything from one of the best nightlife scenes in the world to fabulous beaches to interesting and varied cultural experiences. Miami, with its excellent range of hostels, is a great base or starting point to explore other areas of Florida including nearby Fort Lauderdale, the Everglades or Key West before heading north to Orlando (Disneyworld) or west to Tampa Bay on the Gulf Coast.

Getting There

Car
3.5hrs south of Orlando, 30 mins south of Ft. Lauderdale, and 40 minutes north of Florida City.

Coach
Greyhound (4111 NW 27th St, 305-871-1810) from New York (33hrs), from New Orleans (24hrs).

Rail
Amtrak (8303 NW 37th Ave) from New York (28-31hrs).

From the Airport
The **Airport Flyer** Express Bus (#150) runs to Miami Beach for $2.35 from 6am-11pm; **Taxi** $32 flat rate to South Beach; **SuperShuttle** from $19 (see discount on back cover).

Getting Around
Metrobuses fares are $2.25 o/w, $.60 for a transfer. Exact fare is required or buy an EasyCard. Express buses cost $2.65.

Tri-Rail great for day-trips extending 72 miles from Miami. Popular stops include Hollywood, Ft. Lauderdale, Pompano Beach and Boca Raton. One way fares range from $2.50-$6.90. On weekends, the unlimited Daily Pass costs only $5.

Things to See & Do
Metromover elevated, electric monorail runs a 42-mile loop around downtown Miami for free! Includes stops at Bayside and Government Center. Excellent views of Biscayne Bay and the city.

Miami Art Museum specializing in Latin and Contemporary art. Free admission for students and every 2nd Saturday of the month.

Little Havana the Hispanic enclave of Miami is filled with monuments, shops, and restaurants featuring authentic Cuban food.

Biscayne Nat'l Park snorkeling, swimming, diving, and relaxing are favorite activities of visitors to wildlife-filled Biscayne National Park.

Miami Hostels

Decowalk Hostel & Beach Club
928 Ocean Dr
(305) 531-5511
www.decowalkhostel.com
Looking to soak up the sun while you're in Miami - Deco Walk Hostel is the place to start. It's in the Art Deco district of Miami Beach, across the road from the beach and surrounded by bars, clubs and restaurants.

See their ad inside back cover

Freehand Miami Hostel
2727 Indian Creek Drive
(305) 531-2727
www.thefreehand.com
A comfortable community atmosphere. Both shared and private rooms. Just one block from the beach. Free W-Fi in Rooms and Public Areas. Complimentary Continental Breakfast. Specialty Mixology Bar

See their ad to the right

Tropic's Hostel
1550 Collins Avenue
(305) 531-0361
www.tropicshotel.com
Top Hostel in Miami Beach, Open 24hrs, 1 minute from beach & nightlife. Big swimming pool, clean rooms all with air conditioning, private bath & phone. Online reservations. Dorms from $18.

Everglades Nat'l Park
The 3rd largest national park (1.5 million acres) stretches across the southern tip of Florida. The park's diverse eco-system contains fresh and salt water areas, prairies, forests and swamps.

The Everglades are also home to American alligators and crocodiles, sea turtles, birds, fish and the endangered Florida panther. Make sure you have insect repellent. Lots of it! Florida City is a good base for trips to the park.

The Ernest Coe Visitors Center (305-242-7700), at the main entrance, is located on the eastern side of the park at 40001 Rte. 9336, and is accessed via US1 at Florida City. The entrance is open daily and costs $10/car or $5/person for a 7-day park permit.

Ft. Lauderdale
This fun city is only 30 miles north of Miami. The beaches and clear blue waters make it a great destination for a day or a couple of nights.

Key West
A tropical paradise that sports the southern-most tip of the continental US and is the perfect place to relax all day and party all night.

Orlando
Did you know that Orlando offers more than just theme parks and Disney World? But just in case, the major theme parks include Disney Magic Mtn/Epcot, Wet & Wild, Sea World and the Kennedy Space Center.

Tampa Bay
Located on Florida's west coast, just 1.5 hours west of Orlando and 5 hours north of Miami. Tampa Bay makes for an excellent stop enroute to or from Miami or New Orleans. It's a vibrant city with miles of Gulf of Mexico beachfront.

58

www.bakpakguide.com

Freehand MIAMI

GIVE INTO WANDERLUST

Freehand Miami is a hostel for urban travelers who live by their own rules. Come unwind by the pool, enjoy the local food and beverages and sleep in your choice of shared or private accommodations.

BOOK ONLINE AT **THEFREEHAND.COM**

2727 Indian Creek Dr. • Miami Beach, FL 33140 • (305) 531 2727

info.miami@thefreehand.com **f** /freehandmiami 🐦 📷 @freehandmiami

bakpak ▶▶ **canada**

Canada's West offers laid back cities and tons of rugged, outdoor adventures like hiking, snowboarding, kayaking, mountain biking and camping. Don't miss Vancouver, Whistler, Vancouver Island and Banff. Canada's East, meanwhile, provides sophisticated, populous cities such as Toronto and Montreal, old fishing villages, and early European settlements like Quebec City. In the winter check out the ice hotels, ice fishing and dog sledding.

FEATURED HOSTELS & DESTINATIONS

Kelowna, BC

Kelowna, located on Okanagan Lake, midway between Banff and Vancouver, is the hidden gem of Western Canada. During summer you can hike, bike, play water sports, hit the pubs and even try skydiving! In winter, Kelowna turns into the access city for Big White and Silver Star Ski Resorts.

Kelowna Okanagan Lake Hostel
730 Bernard Avenue
(250) 899-3188 (**7** on map pg 6)
www.kelownaolhostel.com
Friendly, affordable & quality living. In downtown and easy lake access. Private rooms and dorm rooms. All ages and any group sizes. International travelers welcome. Free DIY pancake breakfast & coffee

Victoria, Vancouver Is

This small town with a British feel offers good hostels, fun parties and killer whale expeditions. Victoria is a good jumping off point for exploring Vancouver Island. Locally, don't miss

the Butchart Gardens, whale watching and the Empress Hotel.

Ocean Island Inn | Backpackers | Suites
791 Pandora Avenue, Victoria
(888) 888-4180 (**8** on map pg 6)
www.oceanisland.com
"Ocean Island is more than a hostel, it's an experience - an experience akin to being kidnapped by 100 of your closest friends.."
- Lonely Planet 8th Edition.

Banff, AB

Canada's first national park (3rd worldwide) is located in the Canadian Rockies, east of Vancouver. The Canadian Rockies are breathtaking and tons of adventure activities are on offer here, any time of the year.

Banff International Hostel
449 Banff Ave
(403) 985-7744 (**9** on map pg 6)
www.banffinternationalhostel.com
We are close to downtown. We offer clean and quiet accommodations. A kitchen with walk in fridge, stove etc. is at your disposal.

Montreal, QC

Montréal is the gateway to the beautiful French-speaking province of Québec. Visitors are attracted from all over the world to the city year-round for the major sporting and cultural events, the gastronomy and large number of restaurants, bars, shopping, museums and cinemas.

Alexandrie-Montreal
1750 Amherst
(514) 525-9420 (**10** on map pg 7)
www.alexandrie-montreal.com
Centrally located, Walking distance to all attractions, near bus terminal - save on taxi. Economical because price includes everything -breakfast, laundry phone and internet . (888-525-9420

Le Gite du Plateau Mont Royal
185 Sherbrooke Street East
(514) 284-1276 (**10** on map pg 7)
www.hostelmontreal.com
A century old building with a green rooftop terrace. In downtown Montréal, walking distance to Latin Quarter, Blvd Saint-Laurent, Ave Mont-Royal, Old Montréal. Price includes linen, breakfast, taxes.

WEST TREK TOURS

THE BIGGEST & CHEAPEST PARTY TOURS DEPARTING VANCOUVER

CHOOSE YOUR ADVENTURE:

THE ROCKIES
WHISTLER
SEATTLE
VICTORIA
TOFINO (SEASONAL)
PORTLAND (SEASONAL)
RAFTING (SEASONAL)
SKYDIVING (SEASONAL)

WWW.WESTTREK.COM

WESTTREK

Explore Canada
with over 20 itineraries

Enjoy the flexibility of a
Jump-on, Jump off Pass
or the convenience of
following our lead!

*For Moose West Tours quote discount code Bakpak to get 10% off when booking
online, via email or by phone. For Moose East Tours, please book by phone or email.
Offer not combinable with any other discounts.

Vancouver | Whistler | Kelowna | Banff | Jasper | Tofino | Victoria
Toronto | Montreal | Ottawa | Quebec | Halifax | Algonquin

vancouver

Located just across the border from Washington State, Vancouver is known for its natural sky-line of towering snow-capped mountains. The summits of The Lions, Mount Hollyburn, Grouse Mountain, Mount Seymour and Golden Ears soar thousands of feet above the city. Vancouver offers the perfect combination of multi-cultural city and natural beauty.

Vancouver Hostels	pg 66
Vancouver Map	pg 67

Where is Vancouver
3hrs from Seattle on I-5/Hwy99, 10hrs from Banff, 12hrs from Calgary, 3.5hrs by ferry/bus from Victoria and Nanaimo on Vancouver Island.

Coach, Rail, Ferry & Tours
Greyhound Pacific Central Station (1150 Station St, 604-683-8133) from Seattle (4hrs), from Calgary (15hrs). See their ad on page 67).

Amtrak/Via Rail Pacific Central Station (1150 Station St) from Seattle (3.5hrs).

Moose Travel Network Chinook tour starts in Banff, ends in Vancouver. They also offer 2 to 19 day hop-on, hop-off tours start from Vancouver and explore British Columbia and the Banff area in depth (604-297-0255, see their ad on page 62-63). Get 10% off with discount code "Bakpak"

West Trek offer 1 to 4-day tours from Vancouver to the Canadian Rockies, Vancouver Island, Seattle and Portland. Tours operate in summer and winter (604-408-9378, see their ad on page 61).

Ferry to/from Vancouver Island leaves from Tsawwassen Terminal or from Horseshoe Bay Terminal. Both terminals are about 45 minutes from downtown Vancouver. Ferry costs $15.50Cn one-way.

From the Airport
Public Transport The Sky Train's Canada Line rail to Waterfront Station in downtown Vancouver runs every 6-7 (peak) to 12-20 minutes (off-peak) and costs $2.75Cn o/w plus $5Cn extra from the airport. Taxi $34-36Cn.

Getting Around
TransLink (604-953-3333) includes buses, skytrains and seabuses. Day pass $9.75Cn, single trips $2.75-5.50Cn.

Free Things to See & Do
Grouse Grind 2.9km, 3700ft, free trail to hike up mountain in summer. Skyride r/t and admission is $39.95.

Lynn Canyon Suspension Bridge and Ecology Center (take bus # 228 or 229).

Gastown Walking Tour 90 mins, June-Aug, starts at 2pm (604-683-5650).

Open air nightmarket in **Chinatown** (June-Sept).

Wreck Beach clothing optional, near UBC Campus.

Stanley Park rollerblade, bike, hike, stroll along the 5.5 mile seawall or just relax and enjoy this city oasis.

Must See & Do
Grouse Mountain; Seabus ride across harbor; Stanley Park Seawall stroll; Kitsilano Beach; Granville Island.

Money Saving Tips
Nightlife...many of the hostels have bars and drink specials (Cambie, HI-Vancouver Central, SameSun)

Buy $9.75Cn unlimited day pass for skytrain, seabus and buses around Vancouver

Neighborhoods
Gastown; Yaletown; Chinatown; Granville Street; UBC Campus; North Vancouver

Shopping Areas
South Granville Street; Chinatown; Granville Island Market; Main Street (16-33rd Aves); Robson Street

Day/Overnight Trips
Vancouver serves as a launching point to ski trips Whistler (2hrs); or adventure trips to Victoria, Nanaimo and other Vancouver Island destinations (3hrs bus/ferry)

MOVING ON

Victoria good hostels, fun parties and killer whale expeditions!

Portland a few hours south of Seattle with local brews and Euro feel (pg 44)

BC Interior hop on a tour for an great outdoor (and social) adventure

Calgary home of the Stampede every July. Small town feel in the heart of Alberta

Banff/Lake Louise Banff is great all year round, hiking, biking, skiing

VANCOUVER CANADA'S
#1 HOSTEL DESTINATION!

3 convenient downtown locations, no curfews, no lockouts, 24 hr security, legendary bars on-site
ALL AT GREAT RATES!

THE CAMBIE HOSTELS
EST. 1897

WWW.THECAMBIE.COM

VANCOUVER

300 CAMBIE ST
604.684.6466

515 SEYMOUR ST
604.684.7757

NANAIMO - **VANCOUVER ISLAND**

63 VICTORIA CR
250.754.5323

GET THE LATEST NEWS AND JOIN THE CONVERSATION!
@CAMBIEGASTOWN | #THECAMBIE | FB.COM/CAMBIEGASTOWN

VANCOUVER HOSTELS

Vancouver offers good hostels downtown, by the beach, or near the University of British Columbia (UBC). The city is very easy to get around, so where ever you choose to stay, you'll be able to get the most out of your time there (see page 70 for key to hostel icons).

Cambie Hostel - Gastown
300 Cambie Street
(877) 395-5335
www.thecambie.com
Est. 1897, Located in the heart of historic Gastown district. Legendary pub, bakery, free WIFI in lobby, no cover, member discounts, beds from $17/night with membership card

See their ad on page 65

Cambie Hostel - Seymour St.
515 Seymour Street
(866) 623-8496
www.thecambie.com
Est.1880, Located in the downtown core, legendary sports bar & grill, free WIFI in lobby, live music, kitchen, secure, member discounts, beds from $19/night with membership card.

See their ad on page 65

Patricia Hotel/Pat's Pub & Brew House
403 East Hastings Street
(604) 255-4301
www.patriciahotel.ca
Near Gastown & Downtown. Mention Bakpak Guide for $40 Budget Room Special, 2ppl max. Incl private bathroom, TV, WiFi, 20% off food at onsite brewhouse w/ live music, & free breakfast July-Sept. Transit friendly

YWCA Hotel
733 Beatty Street
(604) 895-5830
www.ywcahotel.com
Newly refurbished YWCA Hotel Vancouver offers a warm welcome to all travellers and is a comfortable, safe and affordable place to stay at the heart of downtown's arts and entertainment scene.

St. Clair Hotel
577 Richards Street
(604) 684-3713
www.sourceenterprises.bc.ca
Down Town at Cathedral Square close to all transportation, restaurants, nightclubs, China Town, Gas Town, A heritage building with a nautical theme. Private rooms starting at $46/night.

Tell them Bakpak Dave sent you!

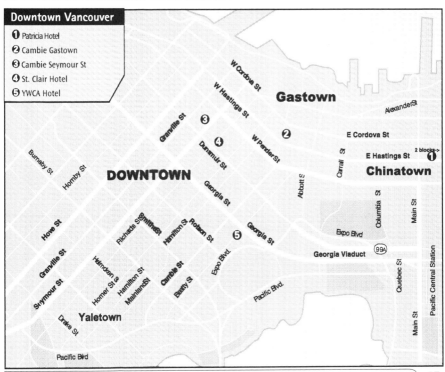

Downtown Vancouver

❶ Patricia Hotel
❷ Cambie Gastown
❸ Cambie Seymour St
❹ St. Clair Hotel
❺ YWCA Hotel

toronto

Canada's largest city, Toronto, is vibrant, cosmopolitan and culturally diverse. On offer are a host of festivals, art, theater and sporting events and international eateries. In the language of the Native North American tribe, the Hurons, Toronto translates into "meeting place." Toronto is a great town to explore by foot or by bike. There are numerous walking and bike paths throughout the city.

Where is Toronto
9hrs north of New York City, 6-7.5 hrs west of Montreal, 5 hrs west of Ottawa, 1 hr from Niagara Falls, 5 hrs from Detroit and 45hrs from Calgary.

Coach, Rail & Tours
Megabus 610 Bay St (www.megabus.com, see their ad to the right), from New York ($23+, 11hrs), from Montreal (from $10, 6hrs) Greyhound 610 Bay St (416-594-1010), New York (12hrs), Montreal (8+hrs), Chicago (12hrs) (see their ad on page 67).

Amtrak (800-872-7245) ViaRail (888-842-7245) arrive/depart from Union Station at 65 Front St.

Moose Travel Network tours of Ontario, Quebec and Niagara Falls from Toronto. Get 10% with discount code "Bakpak" (see their ad pages 62-63)

From the Airport
Public Transport Bus 58A for $3Cn to the Lawrence West stop, transfer to the Yonge-University-Spadina line south to downtown

Shuttle Airport Express Bus to downtown area hotels, $27.95Cn o/w, $42Cn r/t

Taxi about $46Cn, $1-3Cn tip is optional

Getting Around
Toronto Transit (416-393-4636) subway/rapid transit lines, buses and streetcars, 1 trip $3Cn, 3 trips/tokens $8.10Cn, day pass $11Cn for unlimited travel (1 pass covers 2 adults on weekends and holidays)

Toronto Island Ferry $7Cn r/t (416-392-8193) services Centre, Hanlan's Point & Ward Islands from Toronto Ferry Docks at Bay Street and Queens Quay

Hostels in Toronto
Neill-Wycik College Hotel
96 Gerrard Street East
(416) 977-2320
www.neill-wycik.com
Neill-Wycik offers affordable rates in a clean and safe environment in the heart of downtown. Continental Breakfast Included.

See their ad to the right

Free Things to See & Do
City of Toronto Parks offers a series of free self-guided walks that link the city ravines, parks, gardens, beaches and neighborhoods (416-392-1111)

Royal Ontario Museum free 1-2 hours ROMWalk walking tours of Historic Toronto May to Oct (416-586-8097)

CBC Museum (250 Front St West, 416-205-5574)

Bata Shoe Museum Thurs 5-8pm (327 Bloor St West)

Must See & Do
CN Tower; Kensington Market; Second City; Toronto Islands; Hockey Hall of Fame

Money Saving Tips
Theater tickets half price, day-of-show online at www.ToTix.ca or their booth at Yonge-Dundas Square; Transit day pass $11Cn unlimited travel covers 2 adults on weekends and holidays

Neighborhoods
Queen St West (Queen St West b/w Yonge & Bathurst); The Beaches (Queen St East b/w Coxwell & Victoria Park); Greektown (Danforth Ave b/w Chester and Jones); Old Town (bordered by Yonge St, the Don River, Queen St East and the city's railway lines to the south)

Shopping Areas
Kensington Market; St. Lawrence Market; Fashion District (Spadina Ave between Dundas & Front St)

MOVING ON
Montreal gateway to the beautiful French-speaking province of Québec (pg 60)

Niagara Falls spans over 3000 feet and drops over 45 million gallons of water per minute (pg 24)

New York the city that never sleeps. Are you talkin' to me? (pg 48)

Chicago great summer destination, nestled on Lake Michigan (pg 56)

Ottawa will charm you with its European flair, outdoor cafes, markets, Gothic architecture and heritage buildings

See & Stay in LA for One Low Price!

5 Days/4 nights **SUNSHINE DEAL** includes:

☑ 4 Nights LAX Hotel Accommodation
☑ Complete City Tour of Los Angeles
☑ Universal Studios & Disneyland
☑ All Park Entrance fees
☑ All transport to/from Hotel to Parks & LAX

$579 per person (triple/quad occupancy)

BACKPACKER RATES
Packages Save $10
City Tour Save $5

"Everything included except the food!!!"

www.lacitytours.com

email: sales@lacitytours.com

USEFUL #s & METRIC

Lost/Stolen Travellers Checks,
Money Transfers & Currency Exchange

American Express	(800) 221-7282
Thomas Cook	(800) 287-7362
Western Union	(800) 325-6000

Lost/Stolen Credit Cards

American Express	(800) 528-4800
Mastercard	(800) 307-7309
Visa	(800) 847-2911

General Phone Numbers

Emergency	911
Directory Assistance	411
Toll-free Directory	(800) 555-1212

Length	Weight
1 kilometer=0.6 mile	1 kilogram=2.2 pounds
1 mile=1.6 kilometer	1 pound=0.45 kilogram

Mileage	Temperature
30 mph=50 kmh	20F=-7C 32F=0C
50 mph=80 kmh	50F=10C 70F=21C
65 mph=105 kmh	90F=32C

HOSTEL ICONS KEY

Hostels were able to choose up to 5 icons from the following list of 10 to describe their hostel. Some hostels may have more than 5 of the listed services.

- 🏢 **24 hour reception**
- ✈ **Free/Cheap Airport Pick-up**
- 🚆 **Free/Cheap Bus/Rail Pick-up**
- 🛏 **Private Rooms**
- 💻 **Internet Access**
- 📺 **TV/Common Room**
- 🍽 **Free Breakfast**
- 🛏 **Free Linen**
- ☕ **Free Tea & Coffee**
- 🌐 **Tour Desk**

$10 off
any rental

10% off tours

$2 off one-way
$5 off Round trip
Shuttle to NYC

10% off
campervan rentals

$5 off LA City Tours
$10 off LA Packages

$5 off Grand Canyon
Day Tours
$3 off Dorm Beds

$100 off tours

10% off tours

SuperCheap Car
$10 off rentals

Terms & Conditions
Book online at www.supercheapcar.com then redeem coupon when picking up your rental car in Los Angeles, San Francisco or Orange County locations.

See SuperCheap Car's ad on page 17

TrekAmerica
10% off tours

Terms & Conditions
Book online at www.trekamerica.com or call 1-800-873-5872 and use discount code **150260**. Discount applies to new bookings only made directly with TrekAmerica, is valid for new bookings only and cannot be applied retrospectively. Discount cannot be combined with any other promotion. Applicable to scheduled and published departures only.

See TrekAmerica's ad on page 1

Newark Airport Express
$2-5 off shuttle

Terms & Conditions
Present ad on page 52 to Newark Airport Express agents when purchasing your shuttle ticket at any of the following locations: Newark Airport, Grand Central Station, Port Authority Bus Terminal or Bryant Park. Coupon offer is $2 off one-way shuttle service or $5 off round-trip.

See Newark Airport Express ad on page 52

JUCY Campervans
10% off rentals

Terms & Conditions
Book online at www.jucyworld.com or call 1-800-650-4180 and use discount code **BPguide14**. Discount valid for USA rentals for travel between 21 Nov 13 and 31 Jul 2015.

See JUCY's ad on the inside front cover

LA City Tours
$5 off LA City Tours
$10 off LA Packages

Terms & Conditions
Book online at www.lacitytours.com or call 1-888-800-7878 to book a city tour or Los Angeles package. Choose the backpacker/student rates when booking to get your discount.

See LA City Tour's ad on page 70

Grand Canyon Hostel
$5 off Grand Canyon Day Tours
$3 off Dorm Beds

Terms & Conditions
Tour discount can be applied to Grand Canyon and/or Sedona tour Dorm bed discount can be applied to a maximum of 3 nights Limit 1 coupon per person. Book online at www.grandcanyonhostel.com or call 1-888-44-CANYON.

See Grand Canyon Hostel's ad on page 41

Contiki
$100 off tours

Terms & Conditions
Applies to tours of 10 days or longer. Book online at www.contiki.com or call 1-800-CONTIKI and use promo code **BAKPAKDAVE100**. Valid on new bookings only for tours departing between 12/03/2013 and 12/31/2014. Not combinable with other dollar or percentage off promotions.

See Contiki's ad on page 9

Screaming Eagle
10% off tours

Terms & Conditions
Book online at www.screamingeagle.travel or call 1-888-244-6673 and use promo code **BAKPAK**. Valid on new bookings. Not combinable with other promotions.

See Screaming Eagle's ad on page 15

31316929R00044

Made in the USA
Lexington, KY
10 April 2014